For Erin and Marc

MARFA SOUNDING

Edited by
Jennifer Burris & Ida Soulard

Mousse Publishing

Introduction

Seen from the elevated vantage point of Mimms Ranch, Marfa is a small, flat town suspended against the Far West Texas desert plains. Founded as a railroad water stop, it appears a basin without liquid, dust-filled streets encircled by mountains set at a distance. The initial innocuousness of this landscape transfigures at daybreak and at dusk, as well as with time. An alchemy tapped into by artist Donald Judd and his contemporaries via permanent installations that play across the movement of light and shadow: alternatively evoking geological formations, traces of previous peoples, ecological particularities, mangled commodities, violent histories of conflict and surveillance, and techno-industrial promises wrapped inside their misintent.

Now close your eyes and listen. Wind is a constant, as is the metronomic passing of cargo trains. Wooden roofs of former warehouses crackle as they swell with humidity and warp with heat, while truck engines groan at a remove. Doubling the meaning of "sounding" as the act of measurement (primarily used in reference to a body of water) or the preliminary gathering of information prior to action, *Marfa Sounding*—a three-year exploration into the acoustic processes of a specific place—used sound as a frame for understanding how art integrates with, invades, and is in effect produced by its context. At the same time, the spaces of Marfa also became frames for sound as a form of experience set at the intersection of the individual and the collective; an unspooling of meetings both past and present that together situate music's importance within the development of minimalism. Foregrounding shared experience—the coming together of people at a specific place and time, and in relation to the site that enfolds them—music is a vessel through which minimalism must contend with the political as a charged encounter produced in relation to the other.

Marfa Sounding began as a 2015 curatorial residency with Fieldwork Marfa, an international program run by Beaux-Arts Nantes Saint-Nazaire with the University of Houston School of Art and the Geneva School of Art and Design (HEAD). Focusing on ideas of "phase-shifting" in music, particularly as they relate to early experiments in minimalism, this residency started by tracing an encounter between civil libertarian writer Truman Nelson and experimental composer Steve Reich. In 1966, Nelson approached

Reich with ten hours of recorded tape chronicling his research for a book written between the two "long, hot summers" of American civil unrest: a timespan marked by the murder of a black student named James Powell by an off-duty white policeman in Harlem in July 1964, and the armed attack on Marquette Frye in Watts (Los Angeles) in August 1965. A committed Marxist, Nelson's book—titled *The Torture of Mothers*—describes a lesser-known incident known as the "Harlem Six." It weaves its story using transcribed tape recordings in which six black teenagers and their mothers detail a particular experience of police violence and distorted justice through first-person narrative: the beating of pre-teenagers who accidentally tipped over a bushel box of fruit; the false accusation of those same pre-teenagers of murder; the arrest of slightly-older teenage bystanders who intervened; the brutality of prison guards; invasions of family homes by a corrupt police force; indictments for unrelated murders; and the abdication of a fair hearing by a biased public court.

At their first trial, all six of the accused were convicted of murder, after which Nelson organized a collective fundraising effort to support appeal costs. In giving his tapes to Reich, Nelson hoped that the young composer might create a new work in aid of this effort, which ultimately raised the necessary funds for the eventual acquittal of all but one of the boys. Using a technique he developed for magnetic tape the previous year with *It's Gonna Rain*, which exploits minute imperfections in tape machinery to explore how sound waves interact with each other when out of phase, Reich first isolated a single sentence spoken by eighteen-year old Daniel Hamm. Recounting his efforts to be moved from the station house to the hospital after being beaten by the police, Hamm explains how he needed to self-harm in order to demonstrate the extent of prior abuse: "I had to, like, open the bruise up and let some of the bruise blood come out to show them." In Reich's score, Hamm's words gradually discombobulate first into a sequence of directives— come out / show them—before surrendering to abstract sound. By placing this vocal fragment sourced from an experience of systemic racism in America within a formalist structure, Reich deployed a sonic avant-garde to engage political and social realities. Published by Columbia Records in 1966, *Come Out* is Reich's first commercial

6

record and a landmark of what came to be known as minimalist composition; in the terms of his 1968 manifesto, this is "music as gradual process," a linguistic unfolding manifest via duration.

In these ways, *Come Out* became a catalyst for thinking through the power dynamics—the politics—at play in minimalist work. How do process-based structures in both music and art materialize the relationships between formal experimentation with context and temporality, on the one hand, and ideas of community or sociality, on the other? Reich's composition is a bellwether for the ways in which works of art submerge a factious confluence of racial violence, political turmoil, and localized democratic struggle within abstract systems. Endeavoring to tease out such influence in the space of a particular environment that has become, to a large extent, defined by its relationship with the development of minimalism, *Marfa Sounding* used music as a springboard into notions of freedom, anarchy, power, and place. As Reich describes phase-shifting in his 1970 essay "Some Optimistic Predictions": "I realized that this was a solution to what a composer thinks of as a problem of musical structure: how to begin someplace and go somewhere else. This struck me as a way of going through a number of different relationships with the same thing, without ever having any transition. It would be a seamless continuous process."

The planning approach for each of *Marfa Sounding*'s three years started with discussions around the work of a single maker: Alvin Lucier, Anna Halprin, Tarek Atoui. This tripartite structure began with sound in relation to space, expanded to movement in relation to both sound and space, and resolved upon the practice of a multi-faceted artist who translates and adapts the inheritance of such work for a contemporary world. Early conversations quickly foregrounded the extent to which all three practices are open-ended fields for engagement with other musicians, dancers, composers, and sculptors; the programming, in turn, emerged via this understanding of artistic trajectory not as linear movement but as a constellation of influence, a collective monograph. Often it felt as though we were curating networks of mutual interest and shared investment in places, histories, intentions, and ideas. This book, similarly, is neither an exhibition catalogue nor a compendium of minimalism in music, but, rather, an extension of these conversations. Writers from diverse backgrounds—composers, sound theorists, art critics, dance historians, filmmakers, educators, students, curators, and archivists—take the experience of performance as a point of departure for thinking through some of the innumerous directions opened by those intersecting notions of "music" and "minimalism." Many texts approach music from an intentionally non-expert perspective: engaging sound as listeners, laypeople in an arena of methodological specificity and virtuoso expertise. Yet throughout this circuitous movement from the celestial to the spiritual, the landscape to the body, the book consistently returns to a particular understanding of site: an experiment created by and for the people and places of Marfa.

×

On May 26, 2016, Lucier's *Sferics* (1981) opened the program's first year with a nightlong presentation at Fieldwork Marfa's open ranchland, located just east of the town center. Working with fellow composer Pauline Oliveros, Lucier first attempted to record "sferics" (electromagnetic disturbances in the atmosphere) in the late 1960s. These bonks, tweeks, and whistlers ("downward-gliding signals which may last up to two to three seconds") were not made audible to the human ear, however, until his 1981 attempt in the remote mountains of Colorado. For the Marfa incarnation of this work, which Lucier describes as the most successful to date, he worked closely with composer James Fei, who provides insight into the work's technical complexities in his essay "On Sferics." *Sferics* also introduced the specter of Oliveros, who wasn't physically present at *Marfa Sounding* but whose influence was perceptible throughout the long weekend: most notably in a series of concurrent workshops inspired by the Deep Listening Institute and held at Marfa Independent School District. In her intimate remembrance "On Pauline," artist Maria Chávez (who also didn't participate directly, but who had performed earlier that year at Donald Judd's The Block as part of Marfa Myths music festival) recounts how Oliveros remade her way of listening by playing with uncomfortable noise through joyful improvisation. Oliveros passed away in

November 2016, and Chávez's essay stands as a memorial rendered through the shared experience of sonic reconditioning.

This interpellation between collaborators and teachers—Chávez and Oliveros, Lucier and Fei—opens onto the transformational dynamic between cellist Charles Curtis and iconic minimalist composers like Lucier, La Monte Young, and Éliane Radigue. My essay "Compositions for Charles Curtis" examines the significance of these processes of mutual making for each composer's work as well as for a broader art historical rethinking of minimalism as field rather than structure. In Marfa, Curtis performed Radigue's *Naldjorlak I* (2005) at The Chinati Foundation's Chamberlain Building, followed by three of Lucier's works alternatively performed by Curtis and Lucier himself—*I Am Sitting in a Room* (1969), *Charles Curtis* (2005), and *Slices* (2007)—at the Crowley Theater. Responding to these performances, writer Sabrina Tarasoff deploys the context-dependent compositional unfolding of *I Am Sitting in a Room* to understand the complexity of Marfa as site in "Tracks and Traces"; whereas curator Ida Soulard transfigures an interview with Radigue into "her own story," upon the artist's direct request. Not unlike the processes of composing and performing *Naldjorlak*, Soulard's act of writing "Éliane Radigue, Wild Tones" is yet another expression of the composer's desired movement towards oneness.

Marfa Sounding's performative voyage from landscape to totemic white cube and black box returned to the desert for its concluding event: the premiere of Lucier's solo work for cello and wind, *I Remember Morty* (2016), at the Mimms Ranch viewing area. Assisted by sound artist and theorist Erik DeLuca, who led student workshops and did field recording throughout the weekend, Lucier also re-staged his 1969 composition *Vespers* at Mimms in collaboration with three Marfa locals (Crystal Catano, Rob Gungor, and Christine Olejniczak) and a visiting art student from Nantes (Inès Elichondoborde). Translating animal world echolocation to music using a rare device called a Sondol, or sonar-dolphin, this work asks blindfolded performers to find one other by navigating an expansive terrain at sunset using only the rhythmic responses of hand-held pulse generators.

Oscillating between Marfa and Iceland, DeLuca's essay reads as a similarly sensed navigation through obscured histories and territories in its application of Saidiya Hartman's notion of "critical fabulation" (a blending of archival research, fiction, and theory). Primarily used to dissect silences of the archive, particularly when those absences conceal the enduring abuses that lie in the wake of trans-Atlantic slavery, DeLuca's use of Hartman's methodology here intimates how his conception of "Poet Singers"—artists who embody, transmit, and receive poetic interplay between sound, site, and self—are always somehow engaging latent histories of systemic injustice through the practice of making perceptible. As Curtis said of Lucier's music in their joint interview with Marfa Public Radio: "[Y]ou are bringing into a kind of focus for listeners sounds or phenomena that ... exist in nature or in our bodies. ... The real genius of your work is that you are making these things audible for us. You're bringing them into the realm of perception ... a process of revealing or un-concealing of these things that are already there."

×

In its reckoning with the body's precariousness and need for communal support, *Vespers* foreshadowed the following year's focus on choreographer Anna Halprin, whose dance and pedagogical practice—central to the development of minimalism—focuses on conditions of healing and social justice through an engagement with non-theatrical space. In the early 1960s, artists like Robert Morris, musicians like Terry Riley and La Monte Young, and dancers like Yvonne Rainer and Simone Forti all participated in Halprin's legendary summer studios on a redwood deck built amongst Californian trees. These collective workshops sought new systems for generating creativity by emphasizing the simplicity of task-based actions alongside each performer's emotional history. In Halprin's words, such work introduced an idea of dance as the "rhythmic phenomena of the human being reacting to the environment"—be it an airplane hangar, city street, or part of the natural landscape.

Although Halprin advised the development of *Marfa Sounding*'s program, she was unable to travel to Far West Texas. This presented a particular challenge: how to engage a performance artist's work without that artist's presence, and also without falling back on context-inappropriate conventions of the retrospective? In her essay "Anna Halprin, Becoming Legible in Marfa", dance historian Janice Ross redoubles this absence as a generative pretext for critique: an approach that starts "with memory" and moves forward "through the traces and remains of performance." As Ross describes, both curatorial premise and textual frame serve to multiply Anna's body: suspended across the stages of aging and artistic evolution via archival documentation that stretches from 1957 to 2001, footage repurposed in two films by Jacqueline Caux; inhabited as camp in choreographer Stephen Petronio's adaptation of a work "gifted" to him by Halprin, the gender-fluid striptease *The Courtesan and the Crone* (1999); and evoked through both gesture and prop in collaborators Rashaun Mitchell and Silas Riener's new work for Marfa's arid terrain.

Serving as a counterweight to Ross's "writing with a blindfold," critic Wendy Vogel's essay "The Body Wants" surveys the program's scope from the informed perspective of an engaged audience member and participant. Distilling the relationship between choreography and minimalism to a shared preoccupation with a single question—"How does the body register the space between places?"—Vogel's discussion of a community workshop led by dancer Nina Martin also articulates how a physical interrogation of space can open onto the therapeutic possibilities of movement as well as stillness. Dance as a form of healing similarly drives the conversation between filmmaker Andrew Abrahams, who first met Halprin through their shared work with San Francisco's HIV community in the early years of the AIDS epidemic, and educator Cate Cole Schrim. Expanding upon Vogel's text in his questioning of how the body registers spaces not between places but between people, in this text Abrahams describes how cinema can articulate an idea of performance as the embodiment of one's role or work in ritual.

Halprin's collective experience of ritual—in which a dancer's relationship with their own body is inextricable from their relationship with the group—also appeared in Mitchell and Riener's concluding performance. Working with saxophonist Phillip Greenlief and inspired by philosopher Claude Bragdon's ideas regarding

geometry and organic architecture as everyday forms of divine
connection, the dancers incorporated aspects of their surrounding
environment as a means of connecting to the world at large. Yet as
critic Claudia La Rocco elucidates in "Marfa Notebook," this setting
of wind and sandstorms is not necessarily healing; the landscape
here reveals that potential violence which environments always hold.
She writes, "Phillip's nasal passages and lungs and really his whole
body will be wrecked for days: what it is to circular breathe in the
desert." In this way, their improvisational work was an adaptation to
conditions impossible to domesticate: choosing instead to refract
those same conditions against the kaleidoscopic angles of a mirrored
disco ball that punctured the site's fetishistic expanse.

×

Whereas the first two years of *Marfa Sounding* began with artists
whose practices route through the 1960s and into the present,
the final program took as its core the genre-expanding work of
Tarek Atoui: an artist who reimagines the capacities for sound in
contemporary art contexts. However, as Ida Soulard details in
"Tarek Atoui, Feedbacking," in many ways Atoui's practice is also
in direct line with the "progressive emergence of the background as
figure ... in both sound and visual art" that occurred during these
earlier decades. She explains this continuance as follows: "[A]
music that takes into account the specificity of a space or site
(environmental music) and foregrounds the background on which it
unfolds; a practice of composition that uses feedback process as a
motif of organization; and performances that stress their impact on
both performers and audience." An additional correspondence
between Atoui's work and conceptual innovations of the 1960s lies
in a shared mediation between international exchange and intimate
relation. Through projects that intervene in a particular site or
social context, Atoui heightens this dialectic of internationalism
and intimacy by deploying it within the legacy of feedbacking.
In other words: he expands understanding of what a site is, what
background as sonic tool might encompass; he approaches
recursivity as a constantly layered mode of composition that
intertwines recordings, new instrumentation, improvisation, and

"test sessions"; and he reframes durational performance as a process spread across multiple years, geographies, and bodies.

Atoui's Marfa proposition incorporated two instruments created for previous projects: *Sound Boxes* (2015–), a series of minimalist wooden boxes that house field recordings from water-adjacent sites around the world like Athens, Abu Dhabi, Singapore, and Porto; and *0.9* (2016–), an installation of nine monumental bass synthesizers grouped in three and placed under wooden platforms, which together create subsonic psycho-acoustical effects accessible to all forms of hearing. Each of these instruments emerged from intensive periods of collaborative research; for example, *0.9* was developed at Berkeley with Jeffrey Lubow, who reconfigured the installation for Marfa's performance sites, Perrin Meyer, and Greg Niemeyer. A further layering was created when Atoui invited three sound artists—Amma Ateria, Jad Atoui, and Robert Aiki Aubrey Lowe—to play within this extant field. Oscillating between moments of solo and collective improvisation, Atoui's role as conductor routed each performer's distinct acoustic schematic through the Athens and Abu Dhabi *Sound Boxes*, producing a temporal and spatial disjuncture that transported a Texas audience to the harbors of Greece (the concerts were not situated *against*, but appeared to occur *within* the sonic landscape of industrial Athens). This book adheres to such compositional emphasis on each invited artist's work by presenting, within a framing discussion of Atoui's practice, a series of three in-depth conversations that explore their singular methodology and aural formation: Amma Ateria in conversation with Caitlin Murray, Director of Archives and Programs at Judd Foundation; Jad Atoui in conversation with Claire Amiot, Fieldwork Marfa student; and Robert Aiki Aubrey Lowe in conversation with curator Anthony Elms.

These manifold elements (instruments, performers, sites) were slowly brought together over the course of a ten-day residency, during which Atoui also conducted a series of workshops for Marfa's multiple publics. Working with his brother Jad, he introduced biosensors and instruments both digital and analogue to art students from Houston and Nantes and high school students from Marfa Independent School District. Public sessions held at Vizcaino Park's aluminum-roofed outdoor bandshell and within Saint George Hall's brick-walled auditorium solicited performers through interactive presentations. Following these workshops, six members of the community—Claire Amiot, Alan Dickson, Ian Lewis, Christine Olejniczak, Emma Rogers, and Ryan Rooney—signed on to play *0.9* using minimal hand gestures, sensing the instrument's low frequencies through bare feet. This sonic register, experienced as a form of embodiment, created an immersive base for the two concluding concerts, which were held at the same sites as the public workshops. But while Saint George Hall, despite the occasional interruption of a passing cargo train, roughly conformed to the conventions of concert hall or event space, the cement plain of Vizcaino Park's playfield refused the intense amplification of *0.9*'s stadium-level technology. Saturation is impossible in the desert; what remains is a space of relations between people, a community manifest as landscape. As filmmaker and radio producer Ian Lewis writes in "Rain in the Desert", his experience of performing within and listening to Atoui's work foregrounded this "expanse of nearly untraversable space reaching to the horizon" that is Marfa. It revealed the inherent generosity of a place that refuses to inscribe itself into permanence, a trust placed in the continuous process of adaptation.

While *Marfa Sounding* relied on the work, contributions, and talent of many, the following people in particular were vital to its development. Co-Founder and Producer JD DiFabbio was integral at every stage, manifesting early brainstorming sessions into a dynamic multi-year program. *Marfa Sounding* could not have existed without her ingenuity, experience, and drive. Also at Marfa Live Arts, the wonderful Cate Cole Schrim and Emma Rogers were invaluable members of the production team. As Co-Director of Fieldwork Marfa and Co-Curator of the program's final year, Ida Soulard fashioned the multidimensional research and pedagogical platform within which this project was first formed, and against which it all took place. Her astute interventions took every year to a higher level. Finally, my deepest gratitude extends to the artists and writers who made this project possible. Thank you.

Jennifer Burris
Co-Founder and Curator, *Marfa Sounding*

Alvin Lucier

and

Éliane Radigue

with
Charles Curtis

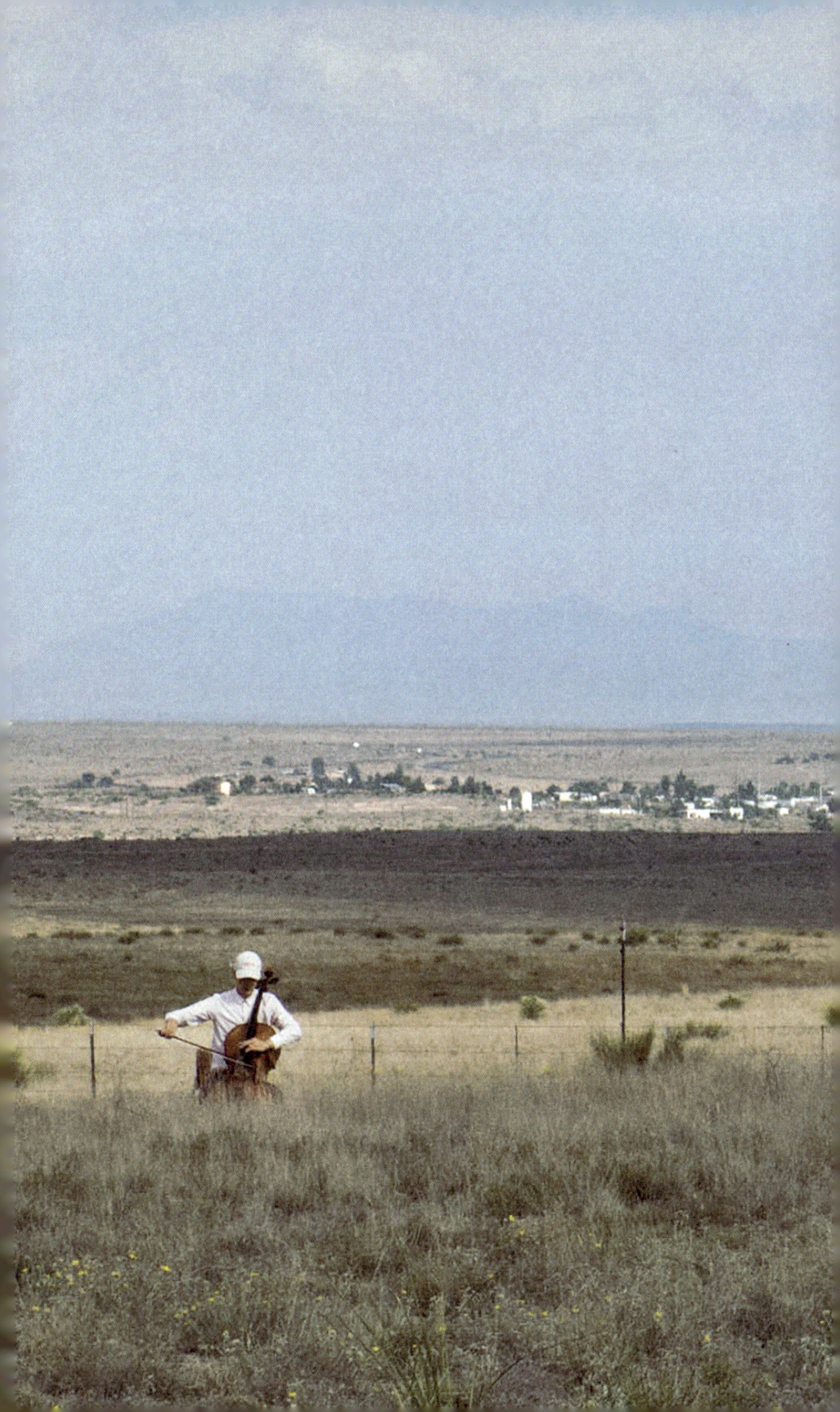

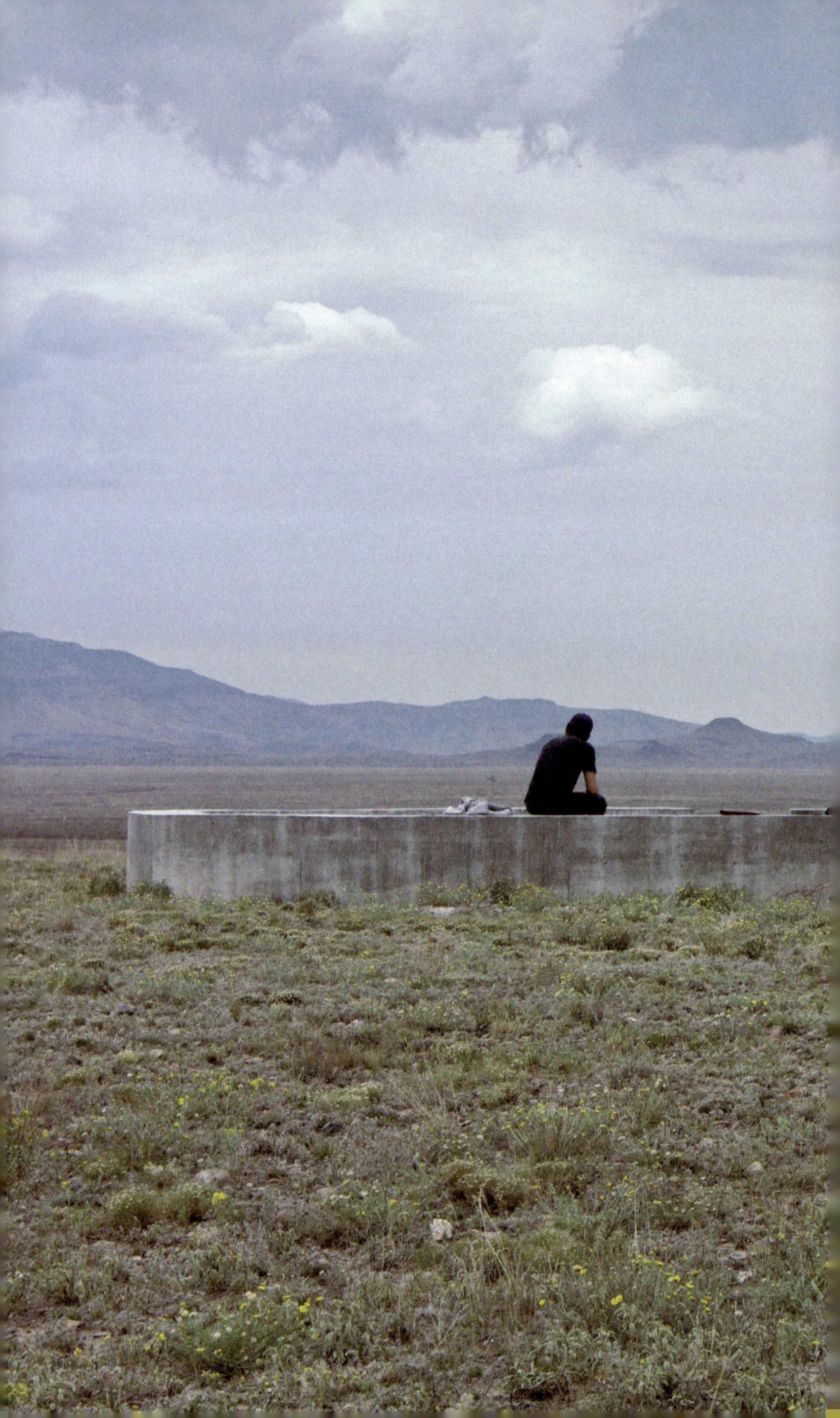

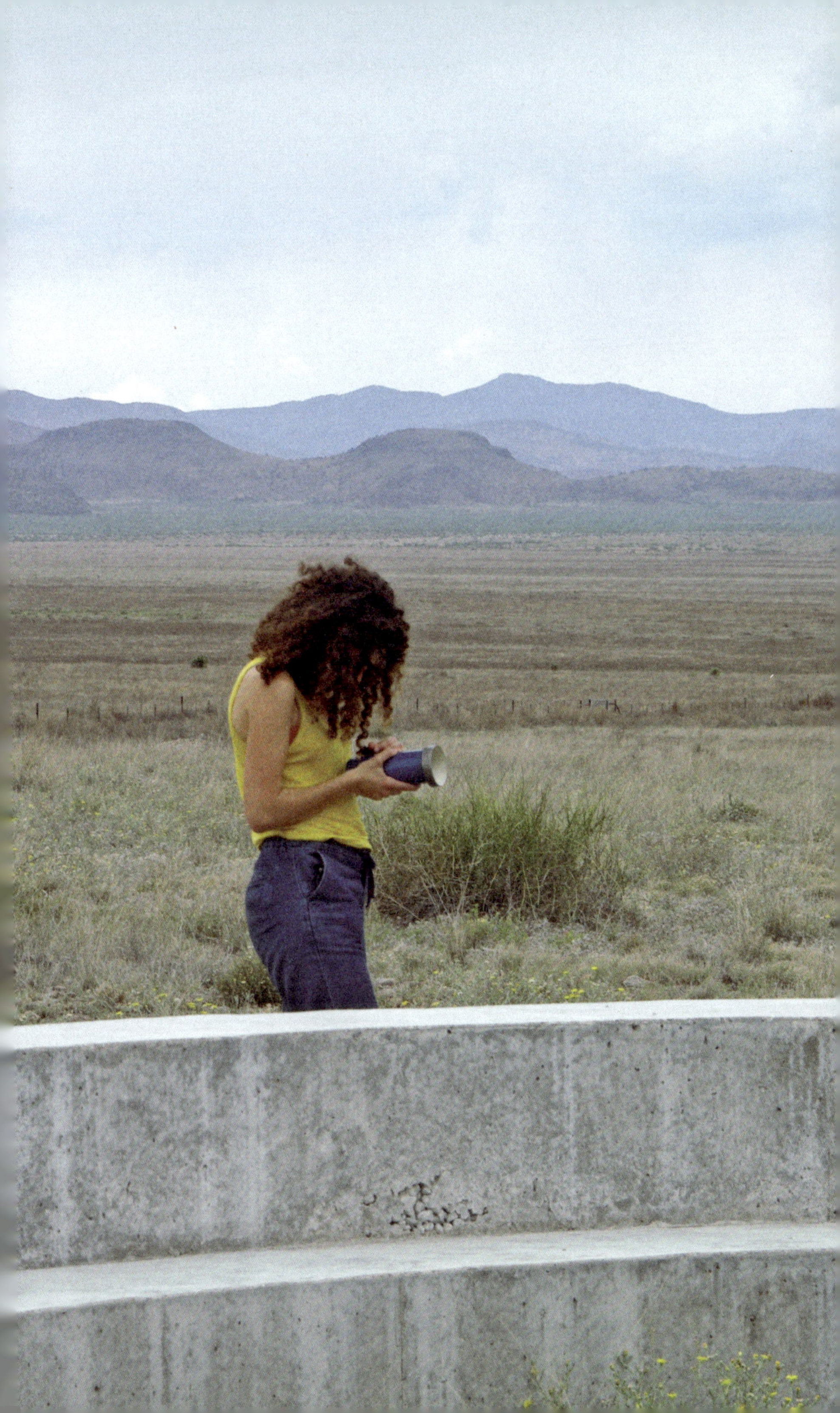

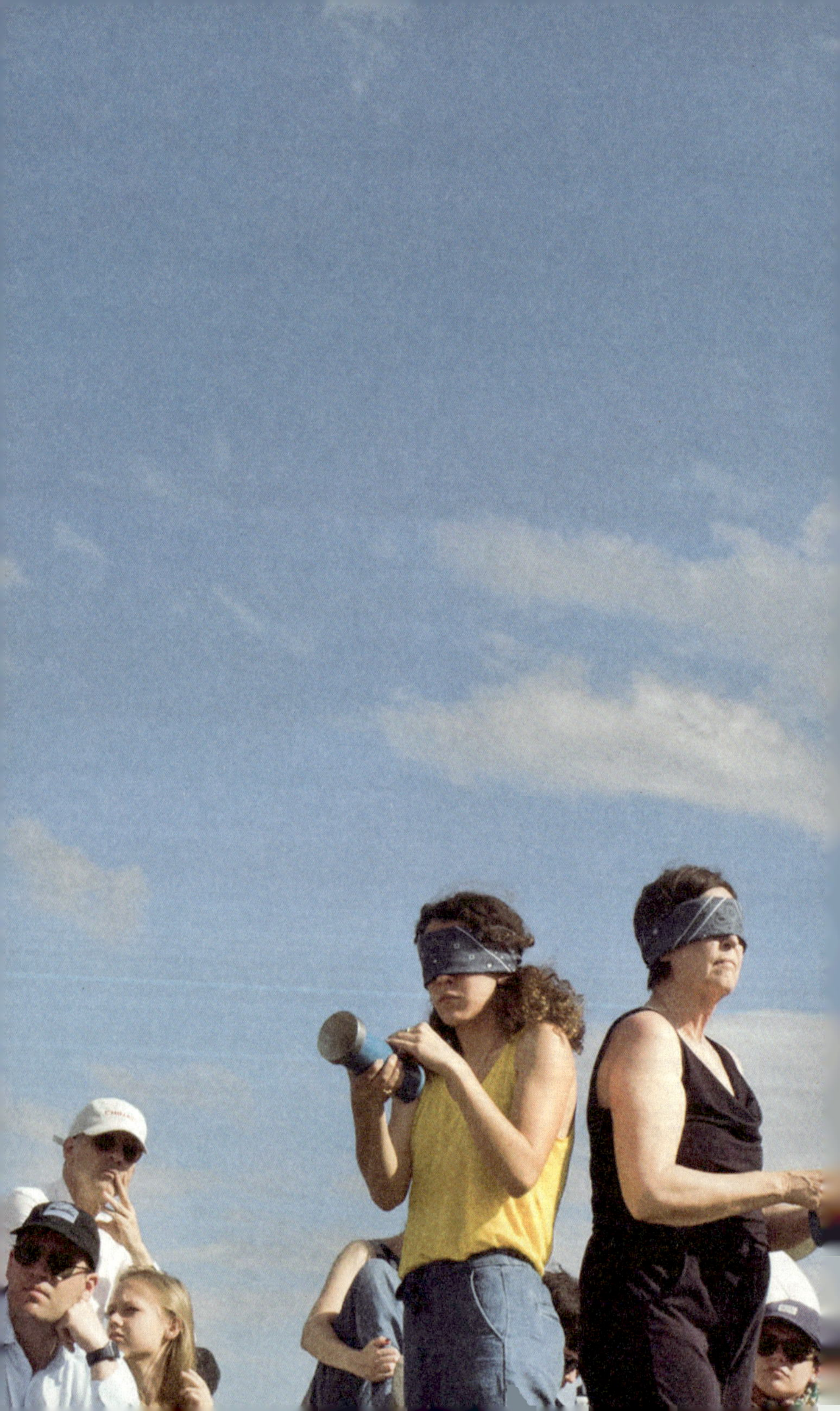

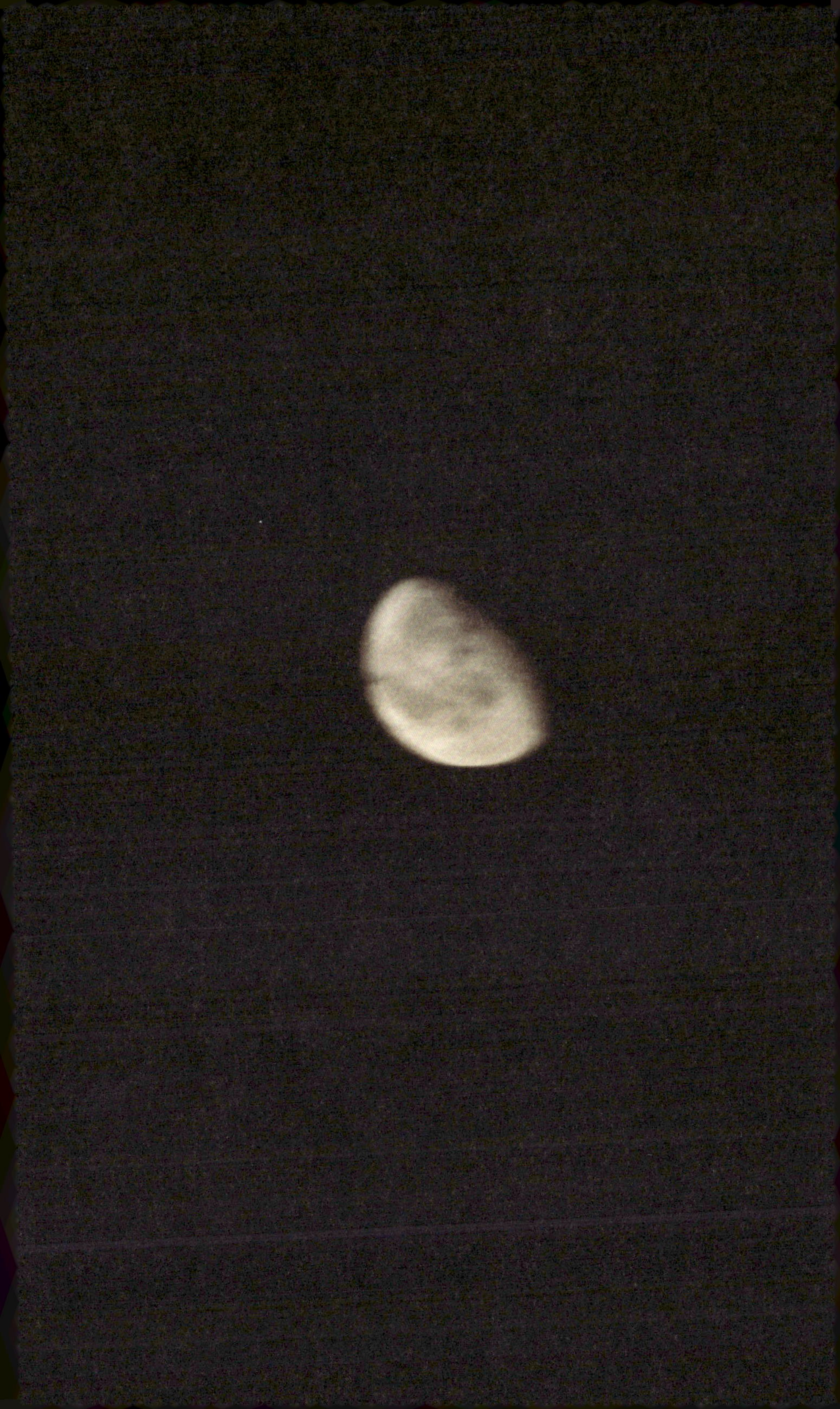

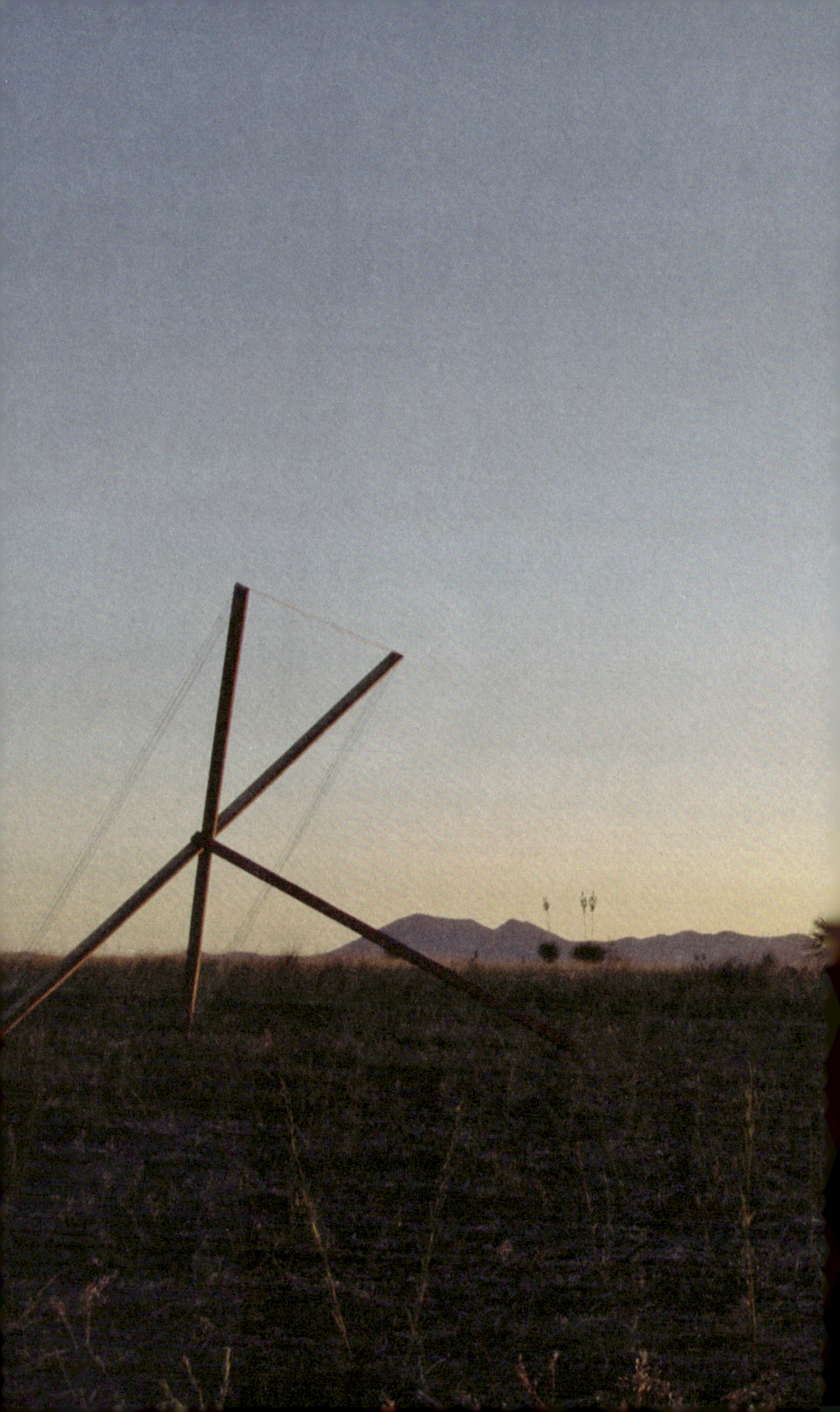

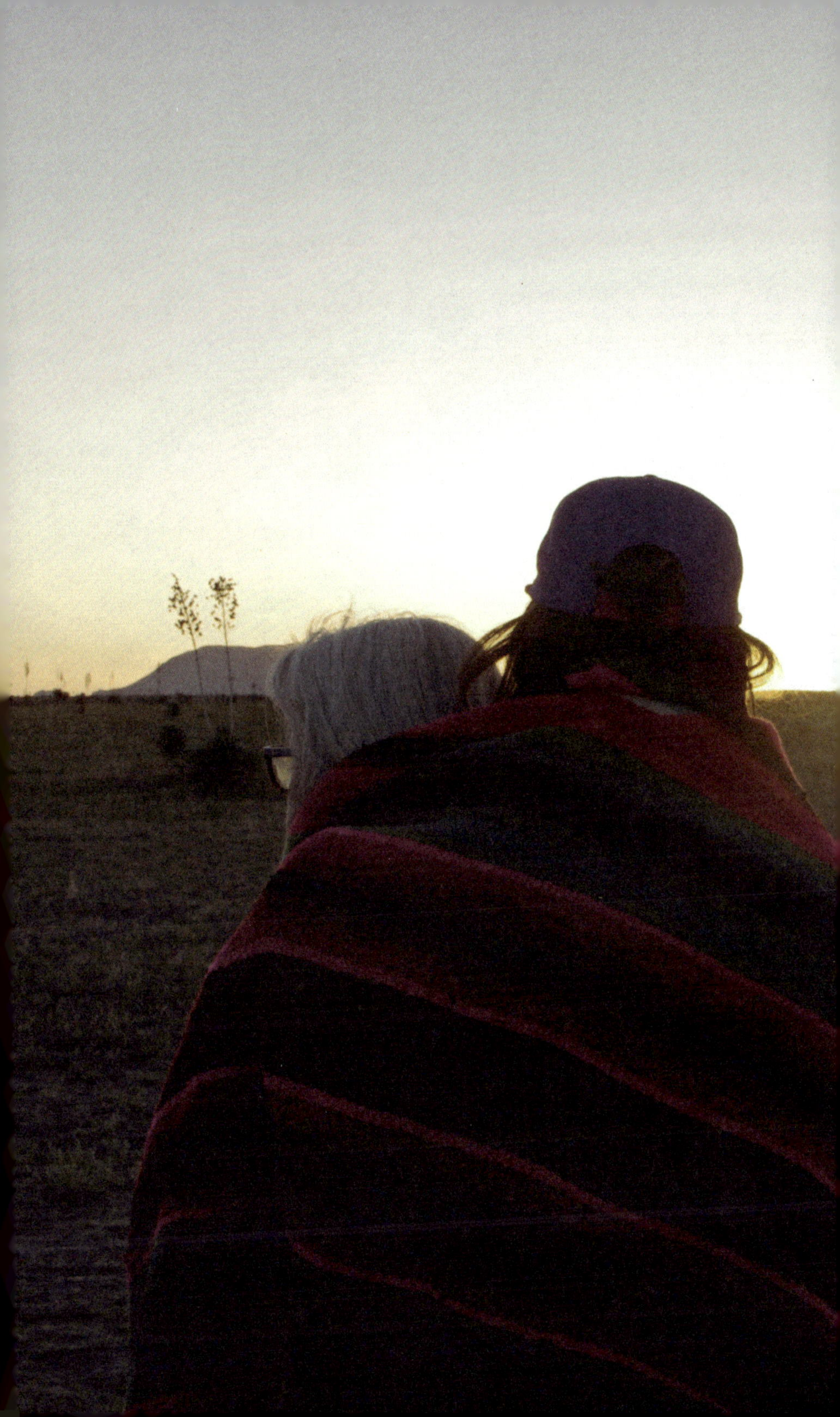

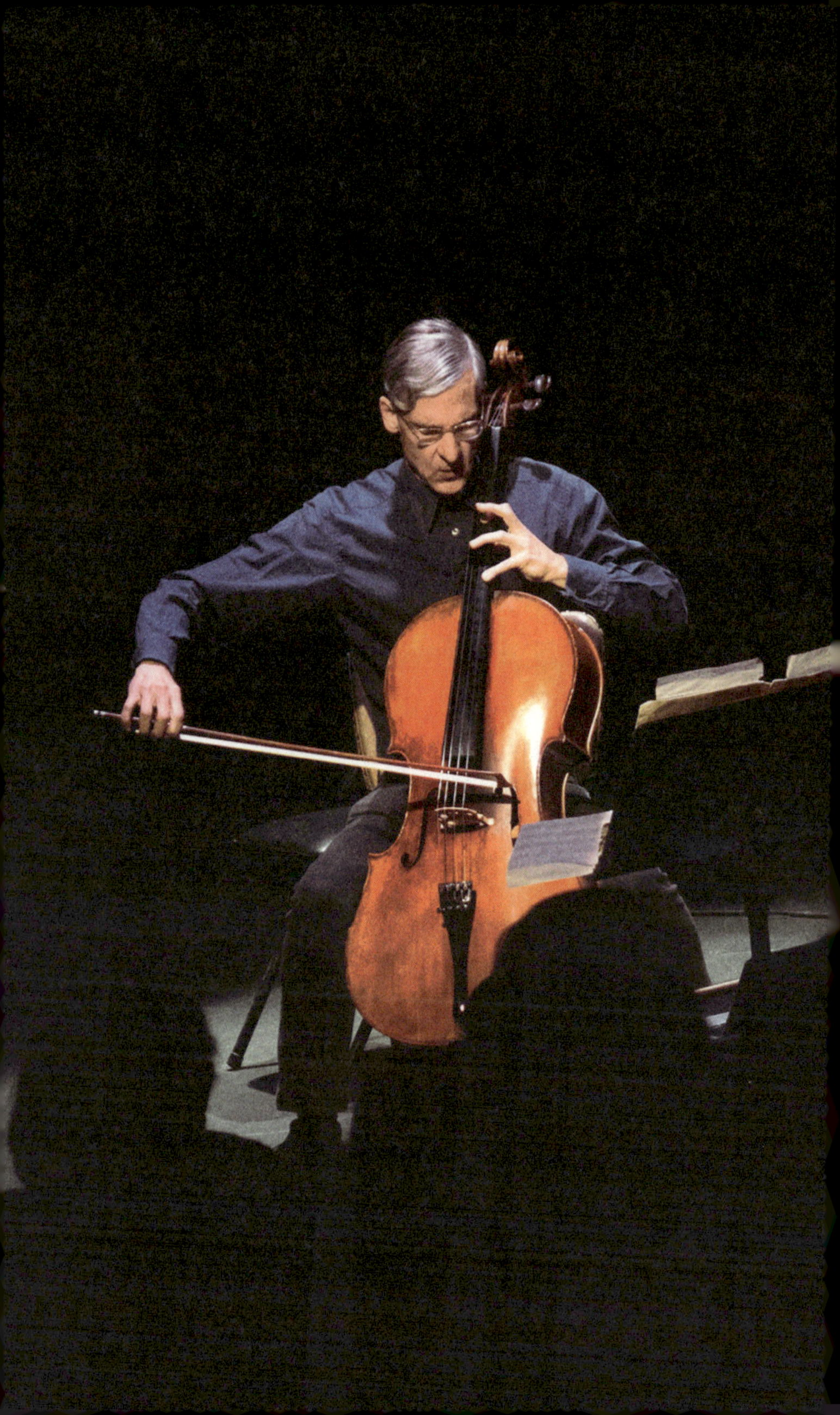

On

Sferics

James Fei

When Alvin Lucier called me about helping him with a show in
Marfa in 2016, he casually mentioned that he'd like to present
Sferics as a live installation. "Do you think it will work?" Frankly,
I wasn't sure at the time.

Sferics captures electrical impulses caused by lightning
discharges, which can travel thousands of miles in the earth's
ionosphere. Depending on the distance traveled, the spectral content
of the impulse can be offset, creating a range of sounds described
as tweeks, bonks, and whistlers. Alvin's original recordings were
recorded in the Colorado mountains in 1981, using a pair of loop
antennas to capture slightly different signals in stereo.

I've been working with Alvin on a variety of pieces since
studying with him at Wesleyan University in the nineties. When the
performances are well done, they seem effortless and stripped of
any superfluous elements, directing the audience's attention solely
to the idea at hand. Achieving this clarity, however, took a great
deal of care, and I was always impressed by Alvin's ability to
instantly identify extraneous material, reducing the presentation
to the essence of the work.

Reviving Alvin's older pieces often required some technical
work. Sometimes electronics needed to be restored (e.g., his alpha
wave amplifier for *Music for Solo Performer* and the galvanic skin
response amplifier for *Clocker*); at other times new software is
created, in the instance of performing *I Am Sitting in a Room* live.
Sferics is particularly problematic because it is so dependent on
the electromagnetic radiation at the location of the installation: the
antennas will pick up any electromagnetic wave, and it is nearly
impossible to avoid the 60Hz hum of electrical power distribution
in most parts of the country. Even in the remote desert site in
Marfa where we were going to install the work, there is a power
line running along the edges. This was trouble.

There are two common ways to pick up Very Low Frequency
radio such as sferics, using either a whip or loop antenna. The
former is more compact and omnidirectional. The loop, while
physically unwieldy, is more directional, rejecting the sides relative
to the front and back by roughly 30dB. This property is critical
in tuning out AC hum and achieving a stereo pickup, and the low

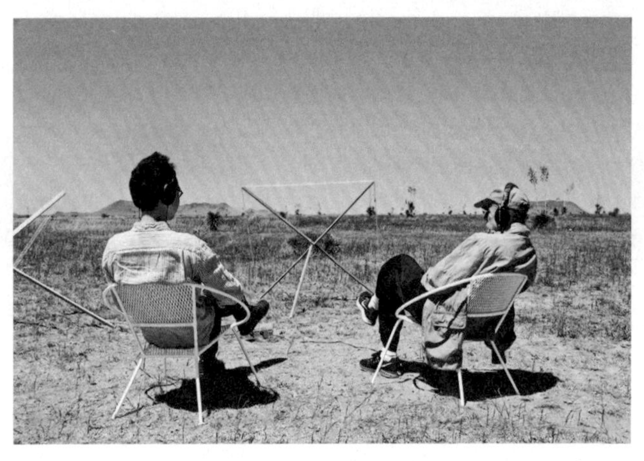

impedance of the loop should theoretically yield a less noisy signal. However, since I wasn't sure how they would turn out until we tested them the day before the installation, I constructed a whip antenna amplifier for Marfa as well, just in case.

Alvin's original antennas were based on a design from Calvin Graf's *Listen to Radio Energy, Light, and Sound*—a cross of 6' pieces of wood with five turns of 22-guage wire evenly spaced apart. The ends of the wire loop are connected to a step-up transformer followed by an amplifier, which were simply the microphone input stages of his tape recorder when Alvin made his Colorado recordings. I replicated this antenna and ran a test in my backyard with a flat microphone preamplifier. My house in Oakland is one block away from the local power substation, so I figured that if I could get any degree of sferics to come through there, it would work fine in Marfa.

The results were not promising: I could barely detect a hint of the characteristic popping static of sferics, and it was so deeply buried under the hum that I wasn't sure about what I was hearing. It became clear that a filter to attenuate the AC-related signal was needed, but figuring out the implementation took some work. I didn't want to use a computer-based system since the installation needed to run for at least 12 hours on battery power in the dessert, and the electromagnetic noise generated by the computer itself can be picked up by the antenna. In order to optimize the filter design, I ended up testing different digital filters on the computer with the very noisy audio recordings I made, balancing the need to reject hum without filtering out the sferics in the process. The most effective setting became the basis of the circuit design, which did yield noisy but passable results in my 60Hz-filled backyard.

Right up until the evening before the installation in Marfa, I had no idea whether the setup would work sufficiently well. With great anxiety, the antennas were assembled under flashlights, located as far away from the power line as possible, and plugged into the amplifier. Much to my relief, sferics came through loud and clear right away. With some adjustments to the orientation of the antenna, it turned out better than anything I could have hoped for. The installation ran overnight, with visitors listening to atmospheric radio as the sun rose in the desert.

Compositions

for

Charles Curtis

Jennifer Burris

On May 29, 2016, Sunday morning, in the high desert plateau of
Marfa, Texas, I received a phone call from the composer Alvin
Lucier in preparation for a performance later that day: the final
event of *Marfa Sounding*'s first year. After visiting the concert venue
earlier in the week, Lucier had suggested we premiere a composition
he would write specifically for the site: a poured concrete
amphitheater, designed by architect Joey Benton for the apex of
a gently-sloped hill at Mimms Ranch's preserved cattle land,
with an acoustic ecology comprised of insects, muffled voices,
constant wind, and echoes of distant planes from a private airfield
situated nearby. However, it was only that morning when, over
the phone, he softly announced that he was ready to dictate the
score: a work he titled *I Remember Morty*.

> In *The King of Denmark*, the performer plays a battery
> of percussion instruments very softly with his or her
> fingertips. Sometimes the sounds are inaudible or hard
> to hear.

> I asked Morty how he got the idea for that piece. He
> said he was sitting on the beach in Far Rockaway,
> Long Island, and he heard wisps of sound, fragments
> of conversation, sounds of transistor radios drawn by
> the wind. They were faraway sounds blown by the wind
> as he was sitting on the beach. In this piece Charles
> Curtis will sit far away from the audience outdoors
> in a windy place. I am hoping that the listener will hear
> fragments of Charles's playing, carried by the wind.

The "Morty" of Lucier's intimate remembrance is American
composer Morton Feldman, who pioneered indeterminate music as
part of an experimental mid-20th century New York group that also
included figures like John Cage, Christian Wolff, and Earle Browne.
In his 2012 book *Music 109: Notes on Experimental Music*, Lucier
describes Feldman's "sound world" as "a quiet one ... Feldman had
very poor eyesight; he was practically blind.... He had to look closely
at things. He had to listen closely to sounds." Feldman's hushed,

slowly evolving music takes form in the 1964 piece *The King of Denmark,* in which a single musician moves through an expanded terrain of percussion instruments that are intermittently played using fingertips, hands, and any part of the arm. This landscape of diverse instrumentation—what composer Stuart Saunders Smiths calls a "percussive ecology"—coupled with the *pianissimo* playing necessitated by the use of fingertips as sounding strike resonates with the wind-tempered acoustics and dispersed field of vision of Mimms Ranch. In a sense, *I Remember Morty* inverses Feldman's original proposition in that the listening experience of disjunct sounds interacting with a landscape's natural resonance—those wisps of transistor radios on the wind—becomes, for Lucier, the work itself; and Feldman's field of percussive ecology created within the space of performance is reimagined as the framing landscape or theatrical field within which the score takes place.

In further describing his affinity for the ways in which Feldman approaches sound, Lucier articulates two key points. First: an emphasis on the surface of things over hidden or transcendent meaning; an approach that Feldman shared with 1950s painters like Philip Guston, Franz Kline, Willem de Kooning, and Mark Rothko: close friends who saw the work's plane—the surface of the canvas, the method of applying paint—as its site of signification. Lucier similarly quotes poet William Carlos Williams's phrase "No ideas but in things" when asked about this approach. And secondly: the importance of quietness, which Lucier further explains in relation to his encounter with the *ch'in* (*qin*) instrument decades later. The *ch'in* is an ancient zither with silk strings that was played during the Ming Dynasty by both scholars and philosophers, often in solitude as a form of meditation. During a lecture-performance of this instrument at Wesleyan by Dr. Tong Kin-Woon, as Lucier recalls, the musician's masterful playing was destroyed by its amplification: tinny loudspeakers and a cheap sound system:

> Between pieces I asked [Dr. Tong] if he wouldn't mind
> playing the next piece unamplified; I wanted to hear
> the *ch'in,* if only once in my life, in its pristine state....
> He replied that we wouldn't be able to hear it. I asked

him what would be so wrong with not hearing one
piece of music among thousands one listens to in
a lifetime.... So he did. It was just gorgeous! You heard
the sound of silk. The audience sat there and leaned
in towards the music.

Back in Marfa, in the bright desert light, Lucier's predilection
for silence, for quiet, was producing a certain level of frustration
as he and cellist Charles Curtis, for whom the score was written,
worked out the intricacies of its materialization. At a distance of
around a hundred yards from the amphitheater, where the audience
would later be seated, Curtis was playing the softest tones audible
while Lucier called out—via a game of spoken telephone—for them
to be even softer: hoping they wouldn't be heard except when the
wind caught and carried them. "The wind doesn't work that way;
Morty was wrong," Curtis replied as a small group of spectators
and assistants crouched in the grass, trying not to interrupt this
migration of whispered sound. Compounding the general mood
was the fact that Marfa's high elevation creates large daily
fluctuations in temperature between day and night, and while the
performance would later take place outdoors as the sun waned,
when the weather was still temperate, the rehearsal took place
across a dry midday heat. As composer and instrumentalist debated
the true acoustical properties of wind from a distance of a hundred
yards, in the desert, via intermediaries who called out their
respective arguments, Curtis's baroque cello was baking in the sun.
Somehow, several hours later, an agreement was reached and the
work was performed just prior to sunset. A small plane from the
nearby airfield, drawn by a large group of people clustered together
in open ranchland staring at a single figure in the distance, circled
overhead: its sounds mixing with what, many in the audience
claimed, was the sound of a cello drawn by the wind. As Cage said
in 1954, "Music is an oversimplification of the situation we actually
are in. An ear alone is not a being: music is one part of theatre."
This experience—the particular process of making *I Remember
Morty*—captures so much of what *Marfa Sounding* intended to
articulate; not just in understanding the centrality of music to the

development of what we now call Minimalism, but also in what
that Minimalism *is*: how it feels, how it is encountered, how
it transfigures and sustains across landscapes and communities,
evading art historical fixations in its slippery emphasis on sensation
and sight. In Lucier's Marfa composition, we find the importance
of place; of an orally-transmitted score imagined for a particular
instrumentalist; a score that is then written through the space
of its performance and the ways in which an audience's diverse
perceptual experiences encounter it; a luxation of ideas across
media both visual and acoustic; and the dispersal of the singular
object into a field of vision, objects, and sounds. As summarized
by philosopher and artist Henry Flynt, a central actor in the
development of these ideas during the 1960s, music is an "arena
for a transformation which did not need to be about music."

In recent years multiple scholars, from Brandon Joseph to
Liz Kotz, have taken up Flynt's claim with rigorous surveys that
examine the extent to which music—specifically as it was reimagined
by Cage and his contemporaries through ideas of event, notation,
and score—became the driving impulse for the development of
a range of artistic movements that took root in the 1960s such as
Minimalism, Post-Minimalism, Fluxus, Process Art, and Land Art.
The intent of *Marfa Sounding*, and this text, is not to replicate
such work, but rather to engage the intimate correspondences and
exchanges through which such relationships play out; in particular,
by focusing on works written by three iconic sound artists—
La Monte Young, Alvin Lucier, and Éliane Radigue—specifically
for, and in many senses with, musician Charles Curtis.

All scores were composed after 2000, a chronology that
pushes against the impulse to chronicle influence via a sequencing
of events. This is standard narrative structure applied to our
understanding of how ideas in art emerge and develop: beginning,
crescendo, end. But if we return to the music itself—those
compositional attempts to dismantle linearity through a radical
refiguring of both time and space within perceptual experience—we
are able to approach "Minimalism" not as a genealogy but as what
Cage called a "field" or "constellation" that artists enter in order
to form intimate correspondences with other artists; what Radigue

describes as "leaving endless freedom to trace one's path, to find one's voice. Pulsations, breaths, beating." How can we translate the embodied experience of listening to a sonic event that not only envelops you, but one that opens onto and interpenetrates other acoustic experiences (that errant plane)? In other words, how do we allow, in Brandon Joseph's words, experimental music's "reconfiguration of the subject-object/listener-work relation into that of a listener within a multidimensional, transformational field" to similarly reconfigure the way in which these experiences, objects, and encounters are presented and understood?

The recurrent node in this essay's rhizomatic tracing is the remarkable cellist and *Marfa Sounding* performer Charles Curtis, who studied with Harvey Shapiro and Leonard Rose at Juilliard, performed as a guest soloist with leading symphonies from Brazil to Florence by way of Carnegie Hall, and migrated through the 1980s New York post-Velvet Underground music scene of clubs and poetry rock before arriving in the realm of just intonation and durational harmonics via his meeting—and resultant long-term collaboration—with experimental composer La Monte Young in 1986. Elements of this ongoing and highly productive correspondence resonate with childhood experiences, as Curtis recounts in a 2010 interview with Natasha Pickowicz. Growing up in the 1960s with a German mother and writer father in, what was then, the countercultural Laguna Beach of coastal California, Curtis would work closely with his pianist-turned-composer brother, who "got the idea that he wanted to be as radical as he could be, as a composer.... And I was sort of his puppet." In high school, the two would listen to vinyl recordings by Cage and Feldman as well as Krzysztof Penderecki and Iannis Xenakis, while Curtis's mother would occasionally play the zither, a German name for a class of traditional stringed instruments, in the kitchen at night: "[I]t's a very soft instrument. It sits on the table and you play it with both hands and it resonates with the surface of the table. And it's very, very quiet....The voice and the strings and the wood of the instrument all resonate together in an incredibly intimate way."

Curtis's early willingness to be, in his own words, "a puppet" for his older sibling later evolved into a highly fluid mode of engaging with composers in the creation of new work. He explains to Pickowicz:

> From my standpoint, it's work that is clearly composed by a composer, but closely in connection to me. It's almost as if my role as interpreter or as performer has bled into the compositional process.... [W]hat has resulted in a few cases with these works that have been made with me is that these works have no existence outside of my performance of them. There is no other performer that can play them.

Such synergy is, as philosopher Édouard Glissant writes in his transformational book *Poetics of Relation*, an encounter "in which each and every identity is extended through a relationship with the Other." The level of critical thoughtfulness and deep engagement that Curtis gives to these collaborations is reflected in the program notes that he frequently writes for performances, as well as in the liner notes he writes for the recordings' commercial release. These notes weave together an account of those experiences of collaborative thinking and working from which the compositions emerge with Curtis's concise articulation, framed by an in-depth knowledge of the cello's harmonics and capacities for different tunings, of each composer's unique contribution to the field of experimental music as articulated through their philosophy of sound. Curtis often takes an invitation to perform as an opportunity to rework these notes: a reiterative process of writing that speaks to the evolution not only of his understanding of the work—an understanding informed by the experience of performance—but of how that experience of performance shifts his memories and conception of the prior experience of collaborative composition.

LA MONTE YOUNG

In 2003 Curtis took a sabbatical from his professorship at the University of California San Diego in order to work with La Monte Young on the development of a new composition: a joint decision that followed nearly two decades of intense association. The two

36

first met in the mid-1980s: a period when Young had left his short,
text-based compositions of the 1960s (the most famous of which
is dedicated to fellow artist Bob Morris and states "Draw a straight
line and follow it") to focus on amplified, sustained drones of pure
sound; and when Curtis was immersed in downtown New York's
alternative music scene. An infamously demanding collaborator,
Young's expectation that his instrumentalists master both a complex
just-intonation tuning process and performance style of extreme
duration resonated with two of Curtis's foundational memories:
first, the intense intimacy of his mother's zither; and secondly, a
fraternal sympathy for an experimental composer. As he explains in
the Pickowicz interview, "[H]ere was La Monte, also asking me
to do outrageous things—but they weren't coming off as outrageous,
they were coming off as *exquisite*.... Without trying to specifically
reference natural sounds or forces, by being in just intonation and
by being so closely related to the harmonic series, these are things
that exist in nature, and the music comes across like a natural
phenomenon, a miracle of nature."

Young wrote *Trio for Strings* (violin, viola, cello) in 1958,
a piece in which a few notes are held for extended periods of time
according to specific intonation and timbral markings. Widely
acknowledged as the first "Minimalist" composition, this piece later
evolved via Curtis's intervention, in which he retroactively applied
Young's own technique of just intonation (which allows for pitch
to be numerically represented via a system of ratios) to change the
work's instrumentation from three to four performers. As Curtis
explains, the very possibility for this type of evolution indicates
how, for Young, "[A]ll of his works constitute one composition, one
single work. He sees his body of work as one work of art.... [T]he
whole thing exists in the present. The whole body of work exists
as a singular moment." In addition to the insight of just intonation,
first suggested to Young by Tony Conrad, this ever-evolving,
singular body of work was intensely influenced by North Indian
vocalist Pandit Pran Nath. A fringe figure even within the world
of 1960s Indian Classic music, Nath's focus was the spiritual
and emotive state or intention of a particular "raga," which can be
briefly explained not as a song but as a melodic framework for

improvisation. First introduced to Nath's music via a recording
shared by musician and spiritual practitioner Shyam Bhatnagar,
Young responded to the apparent similarities between the Kirana
raga and his own interest in sustained, just-tuned harmonies as well
as to Nath's hermetic specificities. For example, during his training
Nath lived for years in the Tapkeshwar Caves and later advocated
a mode of performance in which a particular raga can only be
 sung at a certain time of day. Inviting Nath to New York, Young
became a long-term student and eventual devotee of the master
vocalist; forming the Just Alap Raga Ensemble to further engage
Nath's cosmic approach to raga as transcendent experience via
honorific performances in Europe and the United States.

Drawn more to the technical virtuosity of Young's sonic
atmospherics—as first instrumentalist and later director of the
Theatre of Eternal Music—Curtis had long resisted this religious
dimension, reluctant to "dabble" in a demanding, devotional,
and lifelong practice. He explains in the Pickowicz interview: "[I]n
Indian classical music that term [given] is used more explicitly:
the music is handed down by a guru, who has a spiritual function
as well. The student is a disciple who embodies a very specific
tradition and repertoire of ragas and a very specific set of
techniques." After continuous insistence from Young, however,
of the impossibility of understanding his music without truly
understanding the Kirana *gharana*, Curtis acceded—a shift that
ultimately enabled the solo piece that Young created with him (the
only time he has written a work for a performer other than himself).
Titled *Just Charles and Cello in the Romantic Chord (2002-2003)
in a setting of Abstract #1 (2003) from Quadrilateral Phase Angle
Traversals with Dream Light*, the work can only be performed—like
most of Young's music—in the projected kaleidoscope that is artist
Marian Zazeela's *Dream House*: a continuous integration of the
visual and acoustic expressed through Zazeela and Young's ever-
present partnership.

As Curtis describes in his liner notes for the composition, "La
Monte and I would plot out the composition, I would learn it, he
would compose right in front of me kneeling on the floor, and Marian
was always in the room, with a pencil and paper, listening, drawing,

just being there." Using his vocalist training, Young would sing each individual melody present in the work until Curtis could replicate it perfectly via memory; in the final work the cellist draws on this embodied remembrance of orally-transmitted melodic structure in order to improvise over a series of pre-recorded drones drawn from Young's expansive repertoire of complex rationally-tuned harmonies. This melting of live with electronic sound produces synergistic acoustical effects, an almost biological process that integrates the life experiences of the composer and instrumentalist, the electronic precision of sine waves, and the controlled improvisation of the cello. This isn't a fixed work but a living creature in a way, entirely resistant to inscription as a form of permanence.

The level of control that Young exerts over the entirety of his work, when combined with his focus on the transcendent capacities of durational sound, seems to directly contradict Cage's understanding of freedom as a form of anarchism; that current in Minimalism that decries its innovation as an effect of "everyday objects" constructed through "everyday techniques." As Brandon Joseph explains, "For Cage, the determinate passages from composer to score, score to performer, and performer to listener were understood as power relations. Thus, to disarticulate them as necessary, bi-univocal relations meant that neither performer nor audience member had to be subservient to the will of another: they could instead work from their own centers." This has led some to argue that one of Young's legacies is the re-inscription of control into the field of chance operations and revolutionary techniques, a critique that misapprehends an alternative notion of freedom grounded in devotion rather than ambivalence. It is this particular understanding of a freedom accessed through intense immersion (into a particular acoustic environment, into a tradition of sonic exploration) that has been "given" to Young's artistic practice through his long-term engagement with Indian Classic music.

ALVIN LUCIER

Distinct from Young's focus on the mystical or spiritual properties of durational harmonies, composer Alvin Lucier approaches sound as measurable wavelengths in order to, in his words, transform the "whole idea of music from a metaphor to a fact." These particular strategies of composition emerged in the late 1960s: influenced by conversations with research scientists at MIT, who were focused on new technologies of sound perception and the echolocation processes used by various animal species, as well as by the repetitive movements of Judson Church dancer Trisha Brown, whose straightforward spoken description of these same movements during the performance itself emphasized her rejection of any overlain "artistic" or "poetic" notion. In his program notes Curtis clarifies that, similarly to Trisha Brown, for Lucier:

> Personal expression, expressive gesture, and sound as a rhetorical system take music away from its underlying actuality, the behavior of sound itself. Lucier's early work excludes musical gesture and overt expression in favor of an unparalleled sensitivity to the nuances of sound as it is found in our world. Room acoustics, standing waves and reflections, the physical fact of *wavelength* as opposed to *frequency*, and the limits of our ability to perceive all of this, stand revealed as objects to be contemplated on their own.

Of particular interest to Lucier is the empty vessel or container, which he terms "mediums of music." His work uses emergent technologies of sound modulation in order to draw out the inherent resonance of such mediums—what Curtis describes as the "acoustical signature" of a thimble or a train station—so as to make them audible to the human ear through precise techniques of manipulation. Curtis further details in his program notes: "His subject is the human as listener, and his music can be understood as a detailed, exhaustive investigation into the complexities of the act of listening." In other words, Lucier uses technology to enable us to perceive the existing material properties of everyday acoustics by first amplification and then manipulation through straightforward procedures of displacement, repetition, and gradual change.

Following his initial exclusion, in the 1960s and 70s, of everything associated with the traditional concert hall (notational

scores, symphonic orchestras, instrumentation itself)—as well as of
the conditioned modes of hearing that such associations elicit—
Lucier had, by the early 2000s, begun to integrate the concert hall's
apparatuses with his interest in the unobservable but ever-present
fact of sound in the material everyday. Lucier's first two works
created specifically for the cellist, *Charles Curtis* (2002) and *Slices
for Cello and Pre-Recorded Orchestra* (2011), reveal this re-
engagement with the histories and techniques of European classical
music as he continued to draw forward an idea of composition
intended, as Curtis writes in the program notes for these two
compositions, "[to] capture, reveal, and magnify the details of
 how ordinary sounds behave when we make music." Where the
first work coalesces live performance with slow sweep, pure
wave oscillators, in the second Curtis plays alongside an orchestral
pre-recording of the 53-note cluster of a "virtual cello." At the
Conrad Prebys Concert Hall at U.C. San Diego, instrumentalists
situated alone on stage were individually recorded; each played one
note corresponding to an element in the cello's complete range,
beginning with the low open C string to the high E above the treble
staff. These individual recordings were multi-tracked as loops along
which Curtis plays in performance: as he matches the sustained
note of each orchestral instrumentalist, that note drops away until
the cluster is finally silent—a process of erasure and re-inscription
repeated seven times. Lucier often speaks about his recent
compositions as virtual shapes drawn in air by sound—now
comfortable with placing of abstract forms into the world, where
previously he sought to reveal the natural forms otherwise
unnoticed—and *Slices* can be thought of as a fan that folds and
unfolds with each melodic ordering, the music's wedge and wave
shapes traced by Curtis's deployment of natural harmonics.

ÉLIANE RADIGUE

In 2005, following five solitary decades of working through a
unique form of electronic composition focused on the nuances
of a sustained individual pitch, Radigue created an acoustic
piece for, and in many senses with, Curtis. In her 2006 text, *pour
Charles*, she writes:

The score became the whole body of the instrument.
The result is a kind of wild and frail, versatile and
volatile world of sounds. Taming them with the huge
control that Charles provides all over the piece. The
aim being to follow the natural flowing of overtones
and to respond to the games of the harmonics all
the way up to the threshold of their disappearance
beyond the limits of human hearing.

This composition without a written score marked a decisive
turning point for Éliane Radigue. At the age of 72, following more
than four decades of creating work with electronic media, especially
the ARP 2500 synthesizer coupled with two Revox tape decks,
Radigue began to collaborate with individual musicians: a shift that
has opened up a decade of new compositions for instruments like
the cello, basset horn, harp, bassoon, and viola.

Writing in his program notes for "Éliane Radigue and
Naldjorlak" about the work's formation, a process that took place
over an extended period of working and thinking together at
Radigue's apartment in Paris, Curtis recounts the experience as
"learning to hear as she hears." In Radigue's words, it is a "wonderful
experience of sharing, with the most subtle affinity, complicity."
Such melding of composer with performer explains, in part, the
work's title of *Naldjorlak*: a diminutive of the Tibetan word
referring to the motion of all life toward unity, this coined term is
an attempt to express the intimate or personal embedded in the
movement towards oneness. A Buddhist since the early 1970s, when
she began to study Zen during her decade-long marriage to *nouveau
réaliste* artist Arman, Radigue stopped composing for four years
in 1975 in order to focus exclusively on her spiritual practice. This
intentionality is one of three grounding anchors of her work—the
others being her technical ability to lightly manipulate sounds as a
caress, processes first learned from Pierre Schaffer; and her distinct
auditory capacity for sonic diffusiveness and quiet. Curtis explains:

[Radigue's music] lives not from sound objects
themselves but from their continuous transformation....

She hears sound as spatial ... she hears within a
wide frame of focus in time ... and she hears within
an elongated *now* the change that a sound undergoes
through each moment of change, though presumably
not as discrete moments.... Finally, she hears with
an extraordinarily high tolerance for simultaneous levels
of change and motility, a kind of bravura act of auditory
juggling which results from her unique capacity for
concentration. Most of us experience anxiety when
asked to process simultaneous layers of information;
but Radigue seems to do this naturally, and to seek
this state of multifarious receptivity. Indeed, that
is what seems to guide her along the intricate paths of
her compositions.... [S]he hears *through* her ears
to the infinity that is sound, far beyond what human
ears admit. And her music offers us a glimpse of that.

The title *Naldjorlak* thus expresses both an affectionate
relationship with the philosophical concept of non-dualism found
in Zen and also the compositional attempt for an impossible union:
hearing as another person hears, a melting of sounds between
performer, listener, and site. Such impossibility is further reflected
in the work's use of the so-called "wolf tone." Before each
performance, Curtis spends a day tuning his instrument's strings,
tailpiece, endpin, and tailpiece wire to this "essential frequency of
the cello's resonating cavity": an inherently unstable referent
that changes over time and in response to the physical environment.
Given the intense variability of its anchor, the composition shifts
with every new performance site and within every performance: the
piece is completely and always situational. It is a choreography
that resists written score, presenting sound as both fluid and spatial
and music as entirely dependent on the instrumentalists' embodied
understanding of the composer's auditory landscape. Segmented
in three parts according to the body, mind, and spirit—which roughly
corresponds to the cellist's movement from strings to tailpiece
to spike and ultimately tailpiece wire—this physical enactment of
Naldjorlak makes perceptual the abstracted notion of how we

might, through sound, move towards oneness. Performed in Marfa the same weekend of *I Remember Morty,* at The Chinati Foundation's Chamberlain Building, such qualities included the creaking sounds of the wooden roof in response to the near-constant wind and the occasional passing of freight trains across the train tracks adjacent.

×

Across this small selection of works written for cellist Charles Curtis—other compositions include artist Alison Knowles's *Rice and Beans for Charles Curtis* (2010), for example—we find a distinct relational encounter between those elements that together create a sonic experience: composer, score, instrument, instrumentalist, and the spatial and temporal frame of performance all brought together through the listener's own perceptual encounter, formed, in Curtis's words, not just as "the physiological processing of sound waves [but as] an infinitely complex layering of emotional and cultural responses, memories, habits, preferences, and so on." In the works discussed, a highly specific set of conditions and demands of technical mastery generate the freedom of performance through their very limitations; as Curtis said in his Pinckowicz interview: "[They] push you and prod you to do something you may not have planned to do.... I perform very freely without a score, but I am remembering a kind of a catalog of rules and specific melodic fragments and specific patterns and specific orderings of notes, which is immense. It's an oral tradition." Contained within the field or constellation of perspectives and power relationships that we call Minimalism, whose hard-lined geometries and strict precepts are too often misunderstood as a limiting of that freedom, we instead see how music can open up the possibility to question this perceived dualism of autonomy versus control through its embrace of strict conditions that enable what Curtis calls the melting of sound from "vibration into image, then echo, and finally silence, and after-image." The performer further explains: "The melted state, in contrast to the material state, is not confined to one location, it is all around, and, as image and after-image, in some sense permanent. It is the condition of the physical which is not

44

separate, but continuous with us, and which remains within us."

This poetics of relation found in the intimate correspondence between composer and instrumentalist, and directly influenced by the musical and spiritual traditions like the Kirana gharana and Zen Buddhism, proposes an alternative way of thinking through Minimalism. Not as an aesthetic style, technique, or historically grounded movement, but as a way of deploying artistic practice to upend our perception of temporal continuity and spatial limitation. In Curtis's words—as reiteratively inscribed in his unpublished liner and program notes, a remarkable body of writing that chronicles the process of thinking through and making with another:

> [This] sensibility, this natural affinity for shaping a work to be played by an individual performer, with all his or her subjectivity on full display, into a work *by Radigue* but *for that performer,* has to be accounted as a kind of alchemy. Some kind of turning inside-out of performer-work or performer-score or performer-composer is at play here.... While this notion is given lip-service by countless composers, it functions here in concrete and literal ways.

The Poet

Singers

Erik DeLuca

This speculative essay on in-progress *sound writing* links seemingly unrelated sites (Marfa and Reykjavík), performances (by Solange and Alvin Lucier), and critiques (Donald Judd, the aural avant-garde, and whiteness). But let me explain: *kvæaskapur* is a style of Icelandic folk music: poetry vocalized. In the preface to Icelandic musicologist Hreinn Steingrímsson's book, *Kvæaskapur: Icelandic Epic Song*, Stephen L. Mosko speculates that oral traditions like Icelandic poet singing are unlike broadcast radio because they are not inscribed, recorded, or fixed. They involve the transmission of poetry from the larynx into sites with no architectural resonance (e.g., turf houses). Poet singers remix narratives versified from preexisting prose (e.g., sagas, romances, or novels). However, the *mansöngur*, a short lyrical introduction to each set of verses (*rímnaflokkar*) is an exception. The subject matter of *mansöngur* is the poet's own, most often reflecting their sense of being in the here-and-now. In this context, a poet singer is someone who embodies, transmits, and receives poetic interplay between sound, site, and self.

In the edited collection *Theorizing Sound Writing*, Deborah Kapchan notes that *sound writing* is the performance in word-sound of a "nondiscursive form of affective transmission resulting from acts of listening." This kind of writing—like science fiction, and speculative design—looks toward imaginary futures, between realities, and to posthuman impossibilities: problem finding, question asking, occupying critical parallel worlds of the "unreal" real (i.e., about implication, provocation, humor, ethics, and authorship). One could say it is thought in-progress, in the sense of Anthony Dunne and Fiona Raby's "A/B" (*Speculative Everything Design, Fiction, and Social Dreaming*). Like the propagation of sound in space, progress is to move, advance, develop, grow, improve, and most importantly, process. In a 2018 interview, the poet Eileen Myles discusses process as embodied knowledge. They were prompted to reflect "on experiencing every day as a potential poem." They answered, "[I]t seems like a point of the world. I don't mean so much that the point of the world is to process my writing, but my writing is a way that I process being in the world." I think that I dreamed this: Eileen Myles once told me, "Write from where you are."

I am writing these words traveling at the speed of sound, on a flight to Keflavík. I have been living in Reykjavík for several years, traveling between Iceland and North America. Up here you can touch an otherworldly sense of scale, mobility, capitalist economy, and the post-natural dystopia of the Anthropocene—of "ungrounded transience, of not being at home (or not having a home), of always traversing through elsewhere," as art historian Miwon Kwon says in her article "The Wrong Place". Modes of belonging in the in-between. In *The Queer Art of Failure*, Jack Halberstam writes beautifully about this: "[I]n-between spaces … save us from being snared by the hooks of hegemony and speared by the seductions of the gift shop." Flying over a scene from *Jurassic Park* (that is, the craggy coastline of Greenland), a gift shop passes by my seat, selling glacial salt and geothermal mud, and collecting donations to "Save Icelandic Nature." At moments, connections in this essay might seem far-fetched, because they are. When you come to one of these moments, keep in mind Halberstam's words that "failing, losing, forgetting, unmaking, undoing, unbecoming, not knowing may in fact offer more creative, more cooperative, more surprising ways of being in the world."

This writing also performs as my reflection on the first year of *Marfa Sounding* with Alvin Lucier and Éliane Radigue, a program curated by Jennifer Burris. *Marfa Sounding* is a series of performances, sound installations, film screenings, and conversations that explore the relationship between sound, movement, and the social and geographic specificities of Marfa, Texas. My relationship with Marfa, and my skepticism of Donald Judd, began as a researcher-in-residence at Fieldwork Marfa, an international research program.

The goal is to risk losing one's way. These words are printed on this page, or perhaps appear on your screen, as fixed—still and moving lines of silence—but the writing is not done. In *One Place after Another: Site-Specific Art and Locational Identity*, Miwon Kwon writes:

[T]he operative definition of the site has been transformed from a physical location—grounded, fixed,

actual—to a discursive vector—ungrounded, fluid,
virtual.... [T]he site is now structured (inter)textually
rather than spatially, and its model is not a map
but an itinerary, a fragmentary sequence of events and
actions through spaces, that is, a nomadic narrative
whose path is articulated by the passage of the artist.

×

I'm in Reykjavík, sitting in a room, anchored in the North Atlantic
sea. Down the street, I can visit the fissure between the Eurasian
and North American plates. This geology is recoiling, a work-in-
progress. A digital representation of my voice is being transduced
from a matrix of ones and zeros stored on a computer. These
computer sounds are vibrating up and down a radio transmitter's
antenna. Over my pirate radio station (107.1 FM), a voice—my
voice as radio waves—exits an exhibition space at Listaháskóli
Íslands (the Iceland University of the Arts). At the speed of light,
the waves travel across the road Sæbraut, to the Skarfabakki Pier,
across a portion of Kollafjörður Bay, finally reaching the island
Viðey. This 3.5-kilometer trip takes the radio waves a fraction of
a second, a short echo. Perhaps the composer Pauline Oliveros
would talk about this journey as a kind of computational latency,
time delays resulting from the transmission of data. In *Negotiated
Moments: Improvisation, Sound, and Subjectivity*, Oliveros says:
"[O]ur reality is latency ... the brain tricks us into thinking it's
present, but it's not—it's half a second in the past. We're dealing
with latency all the time."

×

I'm bouncing in the back of a pickup truck with artist James Fei.
The stage seems like the Tarkovsky classic film *Solaris* (1972)—
motionless, mysterious, uncomfortable. We are not on Solaris
though. We are in Far West Texas, Marfa. "Embrace the noise,"
I tell James. "We can't," he replies. James is nervous about the
electromagnetic signals that will come from the power lines.
James explains to me that radio atmospheric signals or *sferics*—
electromagnetic storms in the ionosphere—happen in the same

49

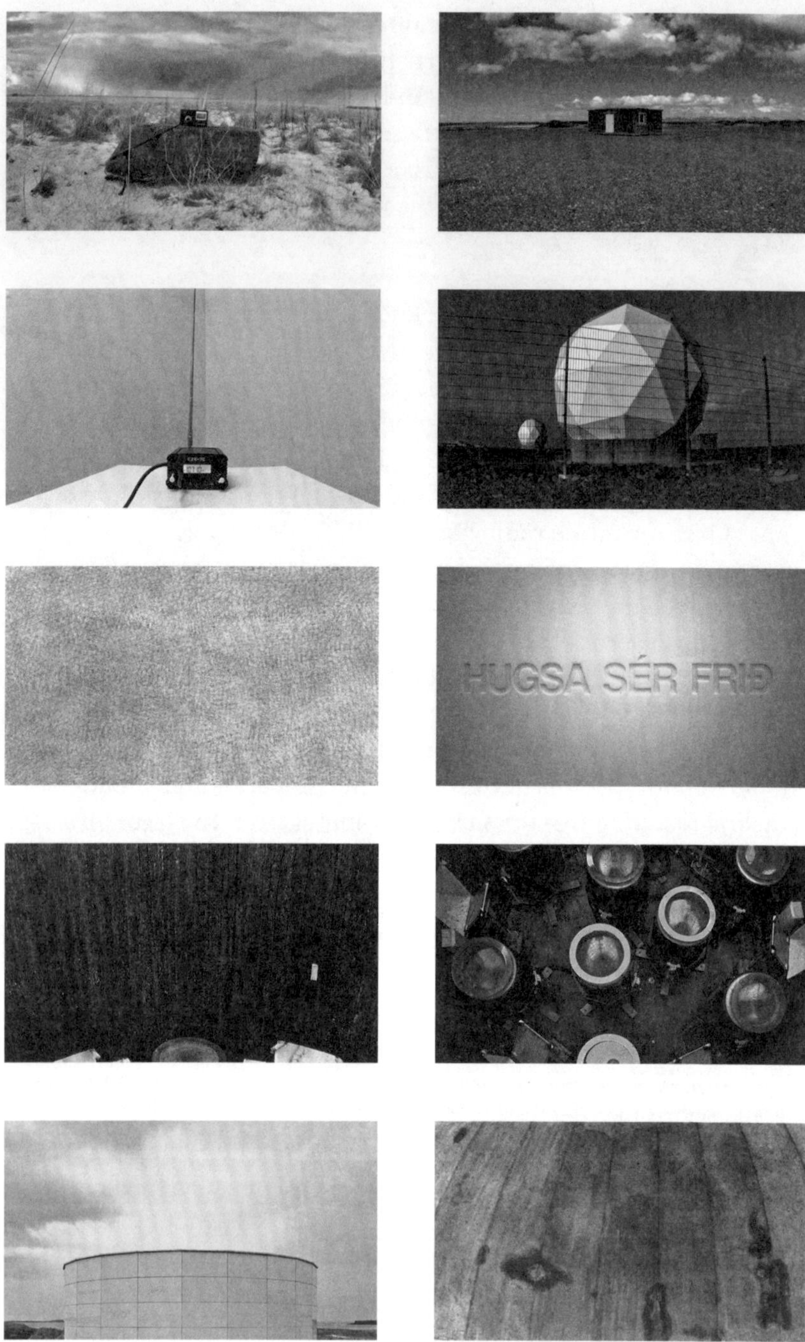
HUGSA SÉR FRIÐ

frequency range of sound, between 500hz and 15,000hz. Sferics are not sound, though; they are magnetic vibrations that can be made audible using the right antenna, amplifier, and filter. In the back of this pickup truck, I feel connected to a NASA-funded effort to make contact with extraterrestrial life. We're not working for some covert operation; we're working for composer Alvin Lucier. It is the first year of *Marfa Sounding*—a project that makes connections between music, architectural space, land use, dedicated fans, and intrigued community members.

×

Between the source of the sound and the reflective surface. Miwon Kwon writes, "It's not a matter of choosing sides ... between the 'wrong' and 'right' places.... [W]e need to be able to think [of] our contradictory desires for them together, at once." Reykjavík, Iceland and Marfa, Texas are 6,629 kilometers apart—0.022 seconds at the speed of light.

×

Friendship, serendipity, sonic specters: I'm sitting in one of those small Fort Russell utility buildings in Marfa. It's Memorial Day weekend, 2016. Icelandic artist Ingólfur Arnarsson draws noise. We are looking at it. In 1992, artist Donald Judd invited Arnarsson to Marfa to install a series of 36 graphite drawings that unfold like a score composed by Morton Feldman. The symmetry in each drawing is ever so slightly different. Tomorrow at Mimms Ranch, Alvin Lucier will premiere a new site-specific composition for the cellist Charles Curtis called *I Remember Morty*. It's a commemorative piece inspired by a story Feldman told Alvin: "He said he was sitting on the beach in Far Rockaway, Long Island, and he heard wisps of sound, fragments of conversation, and sounds of transistor radios drawn by the wind." Feldman hated the radio—not much of a poet singer. About a year after this premiere, I was talking to my new friend, Indra, at the Reykjavík-based art space, Mengi. Out of the blue, I expressed my admiration for Ingólfur Arnarsson's exhibition in Marfa. "Do you know this artist?" I asked Indra. She responded with laughter, "Ingólfur Arnarsson is my husband."

×

I'm back on Viðey island. Today, Yoko Ono lit her outdoor work, *Imagine Peace Tower.* The light bulb produces a tower so big that one can see it anywhere in Reykjavík at night. Eleven hours ago, Ono tweeted, "Art is a concept. Once it's in your memory, no one can destroy it." Yesterday in Marfa, Solange performed her work *Scales* among Judd's 15 untitled works in concrete. Rewind fifty years and a reader of the *New York Times* would find a news item by Pauline Oliveros. She asks, "Why have there been no 'great' women composers?"

×

Alvin Lucier always talks about Pauline Oliveros. In the late 1960s, they zigzagged the La Jolla landscape exploring natural radio frequencies as a kind of real-time performance. In *Software for People* from 1984, Oliveros wrote about this exploration with Lucier:

> I remained hooked on the idea, which seemed to me very poetic: to make an inaudible phenomenon audible, and to reveal and transform that phenomena through artistic intention. How exciting it would have been to actually hear such a powerful natural force as lightning bouncing between earth and the mysterious invisible barrier ionosphere. Since we didn't, the actual result of the performance was not successful, but the intent was lively and imaginative.

There's a new hotel in Marfa called Saint George. When the train passes through Highland Street, the decorations inside vibrate. I watched Alvin notice this as he explained his piece, *Sferics.* Alvin found a how-to book on radio energy, light, and sound. One chapter is on antenna construction. He called an atmospheric lab in Colorado and asked, "How do I get stereo? Do I put one antenna facing the North Pole and one facing the South Pole?" The answer Alvin received: "Sir, we don't deal with stereo."

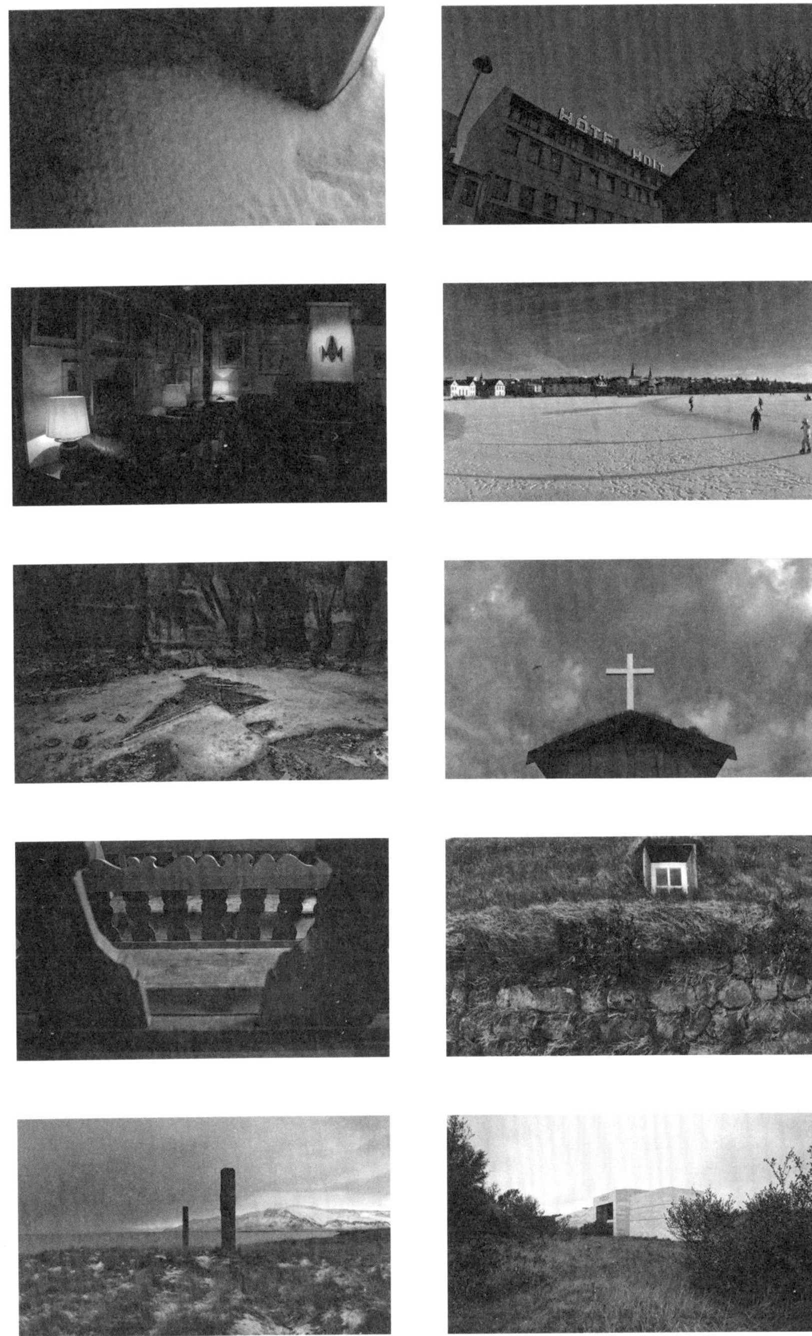

"I remember Donald Judd talking about this," Ingólfur says. We sit in a hotel bar in Reykjavík called Holt. We look at paintings by Jóhannes Sveinsson Kjarval and discuss how the artist Dieter Roth used to bring Ingólfur's studio class here for dinner; how the artists Nam June Paik and Charlotte Moorman gave a controversial Fluxus performance here in 1965, when they were invited by Atli Heimir Sveinsson to perform during the Musica Nova concert series; how pizza didn't arrive on the island, he tells me, until the mid-1970s, fifteen years after Fluxus. "I remember Judd talking about the similarities between West Texas and Iceland," says Ingólfur. "Judd would talk about the low bushy vegetation; the similarities between the sense of scale and space." While the Fluxus inspired SÓM collective challenged Félag Íslenskra Myndlistamanna (the Union for Icelandic Visual Arts), Judd explored the island with his children. The family traced the Icelandic Laxdæla Saga, set in Breiðafjörður out west, and visited landmarks written in the text.

I was talking about the sunshine state with Alvin Lucier. All of the sudden he paused, looked me dead in the eyes and said, "Erik, don't write music that's too busy. If you do, the performer won't be able to listen." That same day I gave a workshop for high school band students in Marfa. They performed Pauline Oliveros's *Sonic Mediation* scores. The students latched onto the idea that music could make them aware of the quotidian flow of everyday life. Oliveros wrote in *Software for People,* "It's not enough just to play the right notes at the right time in the right way; one must also have the right consciousness. This places the performer in the role of explorer of the interior." Like Oliveros, bell hooks in *Teaching to Transgress* writes about exploring the interior: "Home was the place where I was forced to conform to someone else's image of who and what I should be. School was the place where I could forget that self and, through ideas, reinvent myself." In telecommunications, people of power purchase white space (radio frequencies that they don't use) around their desired station to avoid interference. Similarly, John Cage claimed white space

through his practice of silence. In *Keywords in Sound*, Ana María
Ochoa Gautier writes: "Silence is lived as one of the most intense
experiences across cultures." In *Pink Noises: Women on Electronic
Music and Sound*, Tara Rodgers follows: "The function of silence
as a privileged aesthetic category in electronic music discourses
deserves critical attention...[D]espite Cage's own efforts to disrupt
hegemonic silences, the centrality of his work in subsequent
electronic and experimental music histories has often had the
effect of silencing others."

×

Land art, sound, commodification, the wrong place: Donald Judd
was invited to Iceland by Nýlistasafnið (the Living Arts Museum) in
1987. He showed his wall works made of aluminum and plywood.
The two other artists in the show were the walking sculptor
Richard Long and the conceptual artist Kristján Guðmundsson.
At *Marfa Sounding* 2016, the cellist Charles Curtis played Éliane
Radigue's *Naldjorlak* in the Chamberlain Building. This
performance was magic: in-progress sound writing of nondiscursive
knowledge. During this performance, just a mile down Route 67,
Richard Long's *Sea Lava Circles* are just sitting there on a concrete
platform. Still. Not moving. The city of Reykjavík wanted to buy
these circles, but they were too expensive. Judd bought them.
These dead rocks of volcanic change from Iceland sit on an old
tennis court in Marfa. Ingólfur explained to me that the Icelandic
word for stupid, *heimskur*, includes a reference to the word home,
heima. *Skóli* (school); *skór* (shoe); *skol* (o without the apostrophe)
means "a wash." My friend recently taught me two Icelandic
words: *fáviti* and *hálfviti*. *Fáviti* means "knows few things" and
hálfviti means "knows only half of the thing." Expensive rocks in
the wrong place. In Ida Soulard's essay from this book, "Éliane
Radigue, Wild Tones," Radigue says, "There is always, in every
piece I do, something wrong."

×

I think about whiteness in Reykjavík. Not snowy fjord walls, static,
silence, or empty space but the Glacier Mafia—a male, white, rap

crew of, perhaps confused, poet singers. In Iceland I feel like I am
the only one unnerved by the disconnect. A couple months ago
I found myself at a Glacier Mafia concert in a cavernous white box
gallery space. I imagined the group's frontman, Gísli Pálmi, reciting
quotes from Robin DiAngelo's "White Fragility" (2011) to the
audience, and ending with a performance art piece reading bell
hooks' essay "Sexism and Misogyny: Who Takes the Rap?" into
a mirror.

×

We're sitting in a tiny DIY anechoic chamber, a grass-roofed *kirkja*
(church). We are approaching the end of a five-hour opera called
Einfaldsóður written by our buddy Steinni. The tenor in the opera
sings with Kvæðamannafélagið Iðunn (Rímur Society). He's a poet
singer. *Kvæðamaður* means to sing. This style of Icelandic poet
singing was about escapism, a fourteenth century leisure activity.
Each sung poem usually starts with *mansöngur,* or what Steinni
calls "the blog." Perhaps *mansöngur* was an early kind of field
recording about the here-and-now—who left their trash out last
night, town gossip about what Stephen L Mosko calls the
"unrelenting struggle just to survive" with meter, rhythm, and
melody—a kind of local radio station. *Rímnaskáld* is someone who
writes poetry for singing. *Hagyrðingur* is a person who writes
poetry for singing really fast. *Að draga seiminn* is to help a singing
poet breathe by completing their line. *Hestavísur* is horse poetry.
Ólína Andrésdóttir from Flatey wrote a famous *siglingavísur*
(sailing poetry) called *Breiðfirðingavísur. Kveða* is to come up
with a poem and perform it. In *The Importance of Being Iceland:
Travel Essays in Art,* Eileen Myles says that this takes courage.
I would agree. Singing poets are like radio transmitters.

×

Locational, contextualized through Miwon Kwon's paradigms of
site-specificity: phenomenological or experiential (How does an
experience of an art object or event depend on the bodily presence
of a "viewing subject"? How does a work of art become part of, or
restructure the site?); social/institutional (What does a site teach us

about social, economic, and political trajectories?); and discursive
(What is a site? Can it be immaterial? How do "non-sites" delineate
fields of knowledge, intellectual exchange, and/or cultural debate?).
There is a pair of basalt pillars on the northern part of Viðey.
The stones belong to a site-specific sculpture called *Áfangar* (1990)
by artist Richard Serra. Above all, it's an ecotourism destination.
Alvin Lucier testified at Serra's famous *Tilted Arc* trial in the
mid-1980s. He provided evidence that the site of *Tilted Arc* had
optimal acoustics for music performance. Skipping ahead, in a
public conversation held in the bar of Hotel Saint George in Marfa,
Alvin explained, "I didn't know much about what I was doing. I
drove up a mountain road. Set up my two antennas. Put one in one
direction and the other in another to get stereo. I plugged them
into my Sony cassette player. Put on my headphones. And low and
behold, there were these wonderful tweaks and bonks—that's what
scientists call them. I recorded all night long." Certain sferics get
caught on magnetic flux lines and produce whistlers—downward-
gliding signals. Sferics are always happening—right now, they
are there—and in-progress, gliding. This is what Alvin Lucier does.
He taps into things that are happening. This is what Pauline
Oliveros does. She taps into things that are happening. Solange,
Radigue, Myles, hooks, poet singers—they work in-progress.

×

Donald Judd would have become a sound artist—something like
an Icelandic poet singer. As a sound artist, Judd would have
augmented his 100 untitled works in mill aluminum with
a multi-channel sound installation that sonified the boxes' glacial
movement with the weather. The project would have been a
critique of the anthropocene. Judd would have become interested
in sound recording and editing technology to tell stories about
sonic booms and nuclear waste. He would have played his sonic
ethnographies on Marfa Public Radio. He would have worked
with scientists to fabricate new sensors for peering into untold
stories of political power. Like his pal, Walter De Maria,
Judd would have started a noise-rock band. He would have played
drums. Through sound, Judd would have risked losing his way.

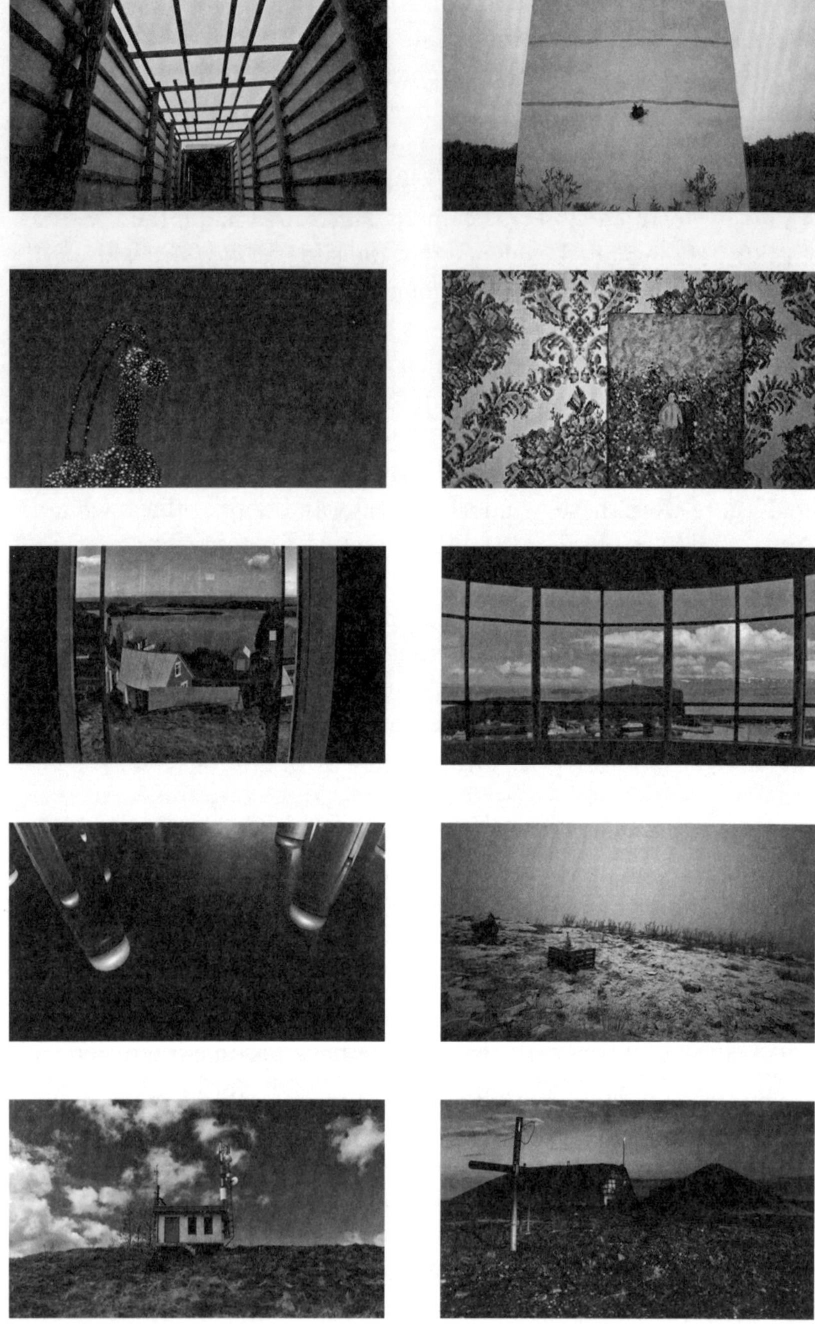

×

Flökkufolk (a nomadic person).

×

The following is a short email correspondence between me and
Alvin Lucier (February 2017):

> [Alvin writes] Dear Erik, Where are you? If you happen
> to be in or near or even plan to be in Florida in the
> near future would you like to help me in an underwater
> project? Please let me know.

> [I respond] Hi Alvin, I'm in Seyðisfjörður, which is a
> small town in east Iceland. I'm working on community
> radio here with the LungA School. I will be in Florida
> in April. Let me know what you are thinking!

> [Alvin writes] Dear Erik, If I mailed you one of my
> precious Sondols would you like to try waterproofing
> it and swim with a dolphin or two in an attempt to
> discover whether or not they recognize it as something
> close to their echolocation language?

In 1969, Alvin wrote the prose score *Vespers*. Blindfolded
performers are asked to echolocate in a space. They use Sondols,
hand-held units that emit short, sharp pulses of sound. The pulses
echo off surfaces. Each echo reveals a little detail of the space: an
acoustic photograph that is comprised of many little pixels of sound
echoes. During *Marfa Sounding*, Vespers was performed in the
sunshine at the outdoor Mimms Ranch desert amphitheater. This
happened on Sunday, May 29th, 2016 at around 5PM EST. Alvin, the
four performers (Crystal Catano, Inès Elichondoborde, Rob Gungor,
and Christine Olejniczak), and I agreed that the work would end
when everyone made their way to the center of the amphitheater.
About twenty-three minutes into the piece, one of the performers got
lost in the brush. Something like Brechtian theater: Alvin whispered,
"What should we do?" I replied, "I think we should go get her." I

slowly walked to the lost performer and guided her back to the
amphitheater. *Vespers* ended and the audience clapped.

×

"An encounter with a 'wrong place' is likely to expose the instability
of the 'right place,' and by extension the instability of the self"
Kwon writes. The ionosphere is a site on the margins but it doesn't
resist—it's more like a "gravel pit of hope" says Lucy Lippard in
*Undermining: A Wild Ride Through Land Use, Politics, and Art in the
Changing West*. I wonder what Judd would have thought about
Solange's performance in Marfa. Eileen Myles explained to me that
Roni Horn's *Library of Water* in Stykkishólmur is like a big sad
aquarium. They also wrote, "It's like if America still looked like the
Hudson River Valley and painters from all over the world kept
coming to paint it.... It's not like I can't understand why the art stars
want to make monuments in Iceland."

×

As a sound artist, Donald Judd would have made audible stacks. He
would have turned the heat crackling metal roof of the Chamberlain
Building into a dialogue of untold West Texas histories. He would
have made heuristic audio documenting the U.S./Mexican border.
He would have used the deteriorating adobe wall around his house
in Marfa as a symbol for renouncing his avoidance of discussing his
politics of power. Judd, like Pauline Oliveros and Maryanne Amacher,
would have started using networked technologies, like telematics,
to perform sound art over the Internet to raise awareness of net
neutrality. He would have collaborated with the Icelandic singer Björk
on an outdoor sound performance about NASA's presence in Iceland.
This new work would have been featured in the philosopher Timothy
Morton's 2018 exhibition, *Hyperobjects*, at Ballroom Marfa. Donald
Judd—as a sound artist—would have worked through his denial and
embraced sound's capacity for allusion and illusion.

×

Someone who embodies, transmits, and receives the poetic
interplay between sound, site, and self. Pauline Oliveros is a poet

singer. Éliane Radigue is a poet singer. Eileen Myles is a poet singer.
bell hooks is a poet singer. Solange is a poet singer. Alvin Lucier
is a poet singer. And perhaps, wherever he is, Donald Judd is now
a poet singer. And yes, the Glacier Mafia push to be poet singers,
but they are lost in the brush.

×

I'm sitting on a wooden bench in Maine with Myles. They say,
"Futurity is OK.... Marfa and Iceland are very related. Right? The
topography, the obscurity, the cultural hotness ... the scale of
these two places moves me in some way." In Eileen's book, *On the
Importance of Being Iceland*, they say, "I'm writing now and
I've always been writing this book.... [T]he motive for collecting,
for writing, is to show the entire approach."

"Eileen," I say, "this is what connects Alvin Lucier and
Pauline Oliveros. In their work, like yours, it feels like it's
happening right now, in-progress—like sferics. All the materials,
methods, and intentions are there." "Right", Eileen replies,
"Buddhists always use the word *intention*.... [Y]ou don't get
there, you don't get it, there is no it, you just see what there is."

Éliane Radigue,

Wild Tones

Ida Soulard

I meet Éliane Radigue, eighty-six, in her apartment, located in a
lively part of the 14th arrondissement in Paris. She tells me this will
be one of the last interviews she gives, as she now feels time is
passing rapidly and wants to concentrate on the only thing that
truly matters to her: new compositional works. She does not want
to be recorded, asking instead that I write my own story. She talks
the way her work unfolds, embarking with the materials, without
any view from above—without system or fixed theory—sliding from
the history of one piece or anecdote to the next with a presence
that permeates. We talk for three hours, share a glass of Porto, and
I leave, highly moved by this encounter, holding her last published
work—*Occam Ocean I* (2014)—in my hands.

×

Solitude is a word that frequently appears in conversation with
Radigue, and a world she seems satisfied to have ultimately left
behind. Her isolated work with the analog ARP synthesizer
parallels her solitude in male-dominated communities: be it with
her former husband Arman and his New Realist friends such
as Yves Klein, Daniel Spoerri, Robert Filliou, Ben Vautier, and
Jacques de la Villeglé; with the two great masters of European
experimental composition, Pierre Henry and Pierre Schaeffer; or
as a single mother of three. "I've always worked very much alone,
except for my cat as an assistant but she didn't say much." This
solitude was an indicator of a practice radically ahead of its time,
which opened uncharted sonic territories. In a way, Radigue's
work can be inscribed within a long modernist tradition of women
working with machines—I think here of those "wives of" working
with woven materials and the early Jacquard machines at the
beginning of the 20th century such as Sonia Delaunay, Anni Albers,
Varvara Stepanova, and Sophie Tauber Arp, among many others.
All of them worked with and through cutting edge technologies,
opening new paths in the visual arts and music. Many are still
under-recognized.

Indeed, Radigue is regularly referred to as a "pioneer woman"
in experimental music, a label which gives her an ambiguous status.
This questionable framing of a pioneer *woman* severs her both from

a general genealogy of experimental music (as a figure of exception)
and from a tradition of music practices carried by women. "Pioneer"
also positions Radigue retroactively as a figure of influence,
highlighting the fact that the works she produced were too forward-
looking for the time in which they were made. It took decades
for them to be properly acknowledged and recognized. "This may be
why," she says, "I started working with live performers at a later
stage.... [N]one of them would have engaged in the kind of music I
was producing [before]."

This language of exceptionalism also feeds upon a practice
that defies simple classification and clear-cut definitions. Radigue's
music is fugitive—neither fully drone nor fully minimal. With no
system or theoretical texts to support a "new definition" of sound,
Radigue insists that her music simply "can express what words
cannot say." It constructs a bridge between two continents and
two aesthetic projects: the European tradition of *musique concrète*,
on the one hand, and the American contemporary scene on the
other, where it was influenced by peers such as Philip Corner,
Philip Glass, Steve Reich, and La Monte Young. She opened her
work quite early to other influences, notably Buddhism, which also
strongly influenced her way of thinking. These various layers
of histories and temporalities are compressed in music that feels
like a long static chant. This compression opens a diagonal path,
taking on experimental histories and traditions like Tibetan or
Mongolian singing, and traces a singular synthetic expression that
evolves into her meditative compositions.

WORKING THROUGH MATERIALS

Radigue doesn't have any *a priori* system, but instead works from
and through materials with extreme rigor and critical awareness.
"There is always, in every piece I do, something wrong," she
says, favoring intuition as a mode of intervention. But the kind
of intuition that Radigue engages is neither superficial nor
subjective; it is conducted not by the immediacy of feelings but by
a specific kind of (non-discursive) knowledge that comes from
and is learned through materials—their constraints and degrees
of freedom. Her place of intervention is what she calls her "tiny

space," a space of maximized constraints that demands a full mastery of its boundaries.

Radigue puts into place the following procedures: logical operations, impersonal flows, and an attention to sonic details in modulation, taking simple elements and pushing them to their highest point of resonance. Her works act like mathematical structures: a series of material inferences that construct and unfold their specific and continuous time-space. But the strict framework within which she works also opens to unexpected results: failures and accidents in which she seems especially interested. These procedures were kept as founding elements once she started, late in life, to work with acoustic instruments: producing spaces of freedom in highly constrained environments.

Opening her music to a new set of constraints, the acoustic world introduced the body of both instrument and performer, responding to these elements with the tools constructed with and through the machine. After more than thirty years of working solely with the ARP 2500, a modular synthesizer, Radigue started a new phase in her practice when Kasper T. Toeplitz, a noise musician, approached her for a commission. It took a long time to convince her, he recalls, but eventually, two years later, their collaboration led to the premiere of *Elemental II* (2005), a composition for double electric bass. "For the first time, a direct interpretation, without any intervention of my old partner, my dear ARP synthesizer, could be realized and offered me the rare and unique pleasure of a living realization, free, and animated only by the talent of its interpreter."

WILD SOUNDS

However, it was not until Radigue collaborated with Charles Curtis on *Naldjorlak* that she decided to fully abandon her long-time partner, the ARP synthesizer, and focus entirely on compositions for live performers. *Naldjorlak* is a three-part piece composed between 2004 and 2009: for a cello (*Naldjorlak I*, Charles Curtis); for two basset horns (*Naldjorlak II*, Carol Robinson and Bruno Martinez); and for two basset horns and cello together (*Naldjorlak III*, Curtis, Robinson, and Martinez). *Naldjorlak I* engages a manipulation of the "wolf tone," the "terror of string instruments

65

performers." The wolf tone is, in the words of Chris Dungey, "the result of the instability between the vibration of the body of the cello and the vibration of the affected string, which then serve to cancel each other out." This can also amplify or expand the frequencies of the original note, creating, as Curtis explains, "an extraordinary spectral complexity." When fully tuned to the wolf tone (tailpiece, spike, and tailpiece wire alike), the cello "behaves somewhat like a bell, or like a tamboura, resonating in a complex but unified fashion."

The use of unstable sounds that respond to their environment is characteristic of Radigue's practice. Those "wild sounds"–*sons sauvages*, as she names them (feedbacks, wolf tone)–suggest a paradoxical mastery of the momentary loss of control of the instrument that create them: a performance from and at the edge of that instrument's specific sensitivity. "It comes from the first access I had to electronic sounds which were the wild sounds coming from feedback. When one sound is coming from one loudspeaker and one microphone it means that when you go too near to the speaker with the microphone everything collapses, and when you go too far, it disappears. If you find the right place, which is very narrow, then you can move it very slowly and it changes but that requires a lot of patience." Those moments of unstable equilibrium, whether with electronic music or live performers, trace a direct line from a practice that dealt with synthetic instruments to the production of an extended synthesis with all the dimensions of live music (instrument, bodies, performer, space).

SPIRIT

The three parts of *Naldjorlak* were created for and with the performers who play them. When creating a new piece, Radigue follows the method she developed with the ARP synthesizer. She begins with a general idea or theme, the "spirit of the piece," which gives way to its structure. *Naldjorlak* is no exception. The title comes from what she calls her semantic "Tibetan cuisine": "*Naljor*" meaning "unity" and "*la*" being a sign of respect. The three parts connect to each other as elements of a whole, which she refers to as the cello being "the body" of the piece and the basset horns its

"voices." Buddhism's dualistic tradition of emptiness and wholeness
is deeply connected to Radigue's durational soundscapes. In the
long and meditative chants she produces, slow modulations and
imperceptibles changes lead to an experience of delayed events.
"Changes *have happened* without even noticing *they were
happening*": infra-modulations altering, progressively and with a
very slow pace, the entire structure. Duration, in Radigue's work,
cuts the chronological time for an experience of floating or being
suspended within a wave of gradual changes. This process is
explained by Radigue through the words of Verlaine: being "never
altogether the same, and never altogether different."

LISTENING

A second moment in Radigue's compositional process lies in
virtuoso listening—very close to fellow experimental composer
Pauline Oliveros's practice of deep listening. Before she met Curtis
in Paris, in 2005, she asked him to provide a "sound catalog"
of his work with the cello. He recalls that "she made her selections
quickly, which she called her 'shopping'.... [T]he sounds and
techniques I proposed I prepared based on their qualities
of diffuseness. I concentrated on sounds which reveal secondary
components at least as prominent as their fundamentals; ...working
with Éliane is learning to hear as she hears." Working with acoustic
instrumentalists did not change Radigue's careful practice of
sound manipulation (the specific performers and instruments were
selected according to this high attention to sonic detail; the two
basset horns, for example, had to be from the same series and maker).
To listen, in her work, means to acquire an in-depth understanding
of the qualities of a specific sound, of what lies between one
sound and another—to "let them live" by accompanying them: a
state of extreme presence, awareness, and patience.

DIALOGUE

Each process of composition similarly emerges from a sustained
conversation with a particular musician or musicians: a back-and-
forth process between the "sonic fantasy of the composer" and its
specific embodiment by performers "who actually make the music."

As Radigue expresses with regards to *Naldjorlak I*: "The score became the whole body of the instrument. The result is a kind of wild and frail, versatile and volatile world of sounds. Taming them with the huge control that Charles provides all over the piece. The aim being to follow the natural flowing of overtones and to respond to the games of the harmonics all the way up to the threshold of their disappearance beyond the limits of human hearing." This one-to-one transmission does not result in any written scores (except for technical notations), but is a continuous choreographic process that apprehends the performer's complete sonic personality.

SITE

To the three dimensions of instrument, performer, and composer, one more element should be added: architecture, or space. Radigue creates "situations;" each performance acts as an "acoustic answer" to a specific space. This expanded experience at the core of Radigue's work parallels what happened in visual arts during the same period. In the 1960 and '70s, the status of the object, whether in society or in art institutions, came under close scrutiny: attention shifting from the autonomy of the object to its context of production, exhibition, and reception. Minimal art instantiated a phenomenological relationship to the artwork, raising awareness of the structural definition of its experience. That era's Light and Space movement similarly acted on the sensorial perception of the spectator. By the mid-1960s art had anchored in a specific site, and context—the background—of the artwork became the new figure.

Site-specificity, as a concept, was formed through the practices and writings of this new generation of artists, among whom Donald Judd produced one of its most refined engagements, at the level of a small West Texas town (despite never stating the term as such). Radigue's work is tied to this idea of "specificity." Her compositions act as sculptural and situational moments. The situations she produces can be understood as a methodological tool that weaves together all the elements contributing to the music piece: its resonance in a specific site, in which the performance space is part of the set-up; the singular ability of each member of the audience to listen to the music, which depends on their level of attention,

concentration, or understanding of the music; and, for acoustic
compositions, the mastery of the performer and the sensitivity of the
instrument. Radigue attempts to reach an experience of synthetic
wholeness: a fleeting union of sound and space.

×

On Friday, May 27, 2016, Charles Curtis performed the first work
in the *Naldjorlak* trilogy at The Chinati Foundation in Marfa, Texas.
A former office and warehouse for the sale of wool and mohair,
the building, made of adobe and tiles with a roof of corrugated
aluminum, contains a permanent installation of twenty-two
sculptures by John Chamberlain. After checking the acoustics
of the space, Curtis decides to sit in a corner. We—teachers and
students from European art schools, members of the Marfa
community, experimental music aficionados, and professionals
from Houston, Los Angeles, and Mexico City—all sit in front
of him. The slow modulations of the cello's wolf tones enter—some
kind of impersonal ritual—in resonance with the surrounding
steel compressions. It felt as though Radigue's world of tones were
being unfolded in their entirety by Curtis's cello. A world of long
duration, patience, continuous transformations, sounds within
sounds, fleeting tones, sounds that emerge between two sounds,
partials, sub-harmonics and overtones, and phenomena of
resonance. The inner richness of a sound and its qualities of
diffusiveness seemed, that day, explored in all their dimensions.

Tracks

and

Traces

Sabrina Tarasoff

To borrow Edward Strickland's words on Alvin Lucier's seminal sound work *I Am Sitting in a Room* (1969), the minute you drive into Marfa, you are no longer an "I" but a "town." The breezy, dusty atmosphere of the city swallows you in its pervasive sense of community, where self seems little more than a "ghostly existence within its resonant frequencies," as Strickland put it in *Minimalism—Origins* (1993). This "I" is absorbed into Marfa's history: the Donald Judd estate, stories of art world heavy-hitters at local saloons, adobe architecture, Chris Wool's studio and, of course, the concrete and aluminum variations of the Judd-founded Chinati Foundation.

In this sense, the *idea* of Marfa, not unlike Raymond Williams's idea of the rural, is based predominantly on social and cultural residue, which is continuously incorporated into its development. It builds on a mythology of exit from noisy urban capitalism but markets this as an experience you can be guided through before grabbing a cocktail. With the distinctions between urban and rural becoming increasingly meaningless, whatever specificity "site" once possessed now seems a catchphrase for local tourism.

This waning notion of "site" was tackled over Memorial Day weekend in May through a series of performances, installations and talks considering the relationship between architecture and electronic music, particularly during the emergence of minimalism. Organized by Jennifer Burris in collaboration with Fieldwork Marfa and Marfa Live Arts, the events of *Marfa Sounding* took place across "sites" as different as a hotel bar and dusty fields, beginning with a dusk-to-dawn excursion to a lone hillside, where a listening station for Lucier's *Sferics* (1981) was installed. The piece converts the notion of long-term observation into sound, with wooden antennae relaying atmospheric interference into headphones. Listening at night, one's body seems detached from one's self, allowing you to focus on sounds as if they are small, abstract thoughts or whimsical notations. Like poetry, *Sferics* claims its dramatic poise by tuning in to material resonances and impulses.

Performed by cellist Charles Curtis, Éliane Radigue's *Naldjorlak (For Charles)* (2006) takes its audience into a similarly indeterminate space—aided, no doubt, by the sweltering hot, dreamlike setting of Chinati's Chamberlain Building. With the cello

71

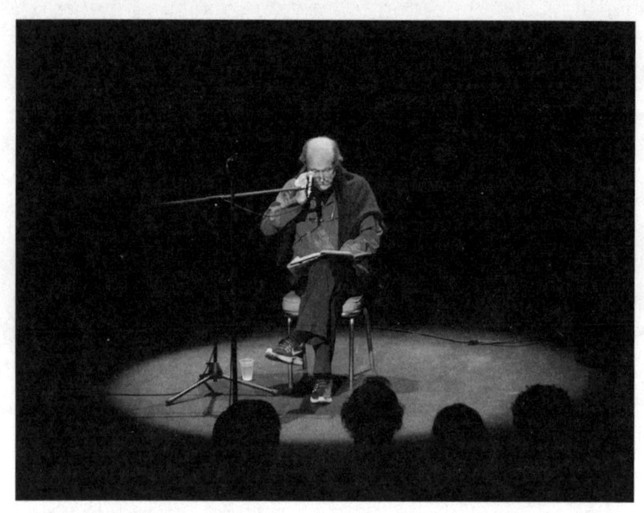

tuned to a "wolf tone" ("the natural frequency of the instrument's resonating cavity"), the piece hones in on those affective spaces caused by oscillating tones, conveying with each note a particular intimacy that the audience is invited to dwell in. You are not *in* the music when you are listening to *Naldjorlak*, but at its edges, observing without judgement and allowing the effects of the piece to be felt.

Fragility was also central to the following day's performance of Lucier's *I Am Sitting in a Room*—a work that breaks apart everything but rhythm, deconstructing the performer's voice into anonymous feedback loops of speech. Experience segues into science fiction, as Lucier eliminates his voice via a repeated process of recording a phrase and replaying it, until all that is left is an echo. The voice, or what is left of it, consigns its personal expression to common ownership, replacing the pressures of *poiesis* with pure, unfiltered communication. According to the composer, the idea was to "smooth out any irregularities" in his speech, giving rise to a fantasy of assimilation on par with the desire to simply disappear in a room. Acquiescing self into synchronous vibrations sounds like breathing a sigh of relief. It also prods at an escapism not unlike Judd's: the break made is into a site that dominant culture cannot, as of yet, quite comprehend.

Still, whether avoiding the burdens of subjectivity or signification, Lucier, extant only in acoustics, reminds of utopia's more totalitarian ideas, such as the hive mind, as it replaces individualism with the dream of a collective voice. That is: not "I" but a "room"—a communal consciousness, minds coalescing in cultural legacy. The murky distinctions between self and other, work and leisure, idealism and authority seem here to fit into a single sentence, which in all of its abstraction is mesmerizing to dwell in—not unlike Marfa itself, whether browsing through an art bookshop in a boutique hotel or star-gazing from a picnic blanket at the Judd Foundation.

For Pauline

Maria Chávez

Pauline Oliveros and I used to always find our conversations coming back to similar topics about individual perspective in sound and how personal experience shapes the sound we choose to hear or listen to. I always felt that the purpose of my work was to question why we believe certain sounds come off as wrong and ask if there was a way for the "wrong sound" to redeem itself? Beyond the idea of "wrong sounds," there is also the question of personal experience with sound and how one treats those sounds with favorability (i.e., nostalgia) or with rejection (i.e., certain genre of music that is not favorable). This kind of mind conditioning can be seen as happening on all fronts, from the people we grew up with to the community we live in and, of course, how our personal tastes within these genres play out when it comes to the music industry.

Within these contexts, I began to think of a speech that Pauline gave, reminding me of what I consider in my sonic expectations within society. In 2015, Pauline and I were both booked in Belfast to perform as part of a symposium on improvisation and how it can improve child protective services: "Just Improvisation: Enriching child protection law through musical techniques, discourses and pedagogies."

Pauline was there to perform and give the keynote speech "Safe to Play." She began with the always simple yet poignant opening words, "We come into the world ready to play.... Improvisation implies some kind of relationship with play.... The primary plaything is voice. There are no rules for primary improvisation.... Voice is power." She continued. "A loud shriek of frustration is unmistakable.... Sounds are the language of emotions."

As she went on with her keynote I was reminded of a scenario I like to bring up in my lectures about listening and improvisation:

As children, when we play, we are still developing our understanding of our size in relationship to a room. Sometimes, we play too rough and may end up bumping into things. Take the scenario of a child running in a narrow hallway. The hallway could have an end table with a ceramic or glass vase on it. The child, running wild, deep in the act of play, by chance, by accident, bumps into the table at a speed that knocks the vase off its base.

What happens next? The story is all too familiar to many of us.

The vase falls and crashes onto the floor, shattering into pieces. This loud, shattering sound is followed by another loud sound: the sound of the parent or guardian who is now yelling at the child for breaking something that has a value. A value that is unbeknownst to the child.

What child understands value when they are wild with the sense of play?

"The imposition of RULES for play creates the many games and styles that we experience in life. Rules also make it possible to be wrong and unsafe. Ability to learn and follow rules can also bring a sense of safety and accomplishment provided that the rules are taught in a loving way," Pauline continued.

After the lecture, Pauline, her partner Ione, and I had dinner at a nearby restaurant and I applauded her on her lecture. She was skeptical of my praise, always challenging me, as mentors do, and asked what exactly I liked about it.

"I like that you gave children a chance. That you allowed them to play," I said.

I went on to tell her the scenario of the wild child running through a hallway, breaking the vase.

I explained, "When the parent raises their voice in an aggressive manner, following the loud crash of the vase, they have immediately given the sound of the crash a negative meaning. For the rest of that child's life, when they hear the sound of glass crashing they will think that the sound is wrong. The sound of something changing its shape is wrong."

Pauline agreed, to my relief.

Individual experience and perspective shape our sonic lives yet can also confine us to the senses. As with the child that has now assigned the crash of glass to represent a negative scenario, the child grows up only to be greeted with similar crashing glass sounds that are being perpetuated in movies and television: most likely with a negative event occurring due to the crash.

This kind of sonic cultivation is one of many that is constantly overlooked by the media, which can be deemed as highly irresponsible since the media holds a monopoly on sound effects for the purpose of selling stories (cartoons, TV episodes, music).

As the child grows, the individual's ear that is trained to hear and to listen will no doubt begin to attach a memory to a popular song, thereby giving that song more importance in one's memory than others, simply due to experience. One may attach a feeling to an entire genre of music that then creates market for radio stations, online and other, to make stations as what I call "sonic manipulators," or as we all call it, the Oldies stations. While the media has gotten a stronghold on how to manipulate nostalgia while abusing sound effects to sell stories, the responsibility still falls on the individual.

Pauline helped me further these ideas on individual perspective in sound, reminding me to not just look at the content of hearing/listening but also at the amplitude, dynamics, and volume that the sounds are being pushed through.

What of the majority of humans who are constantly surrounded by powered amplification during this time in our history? Whether it is through small earbuds or when one is in a car listening to the radio or amplified speakers in stores, in the 21st Century, amplification is the way the world listens. A measurable volume now has the ability to determine the legitimacy of a sound. This type of legitimizing tends to allow the listener to confine the senses.

My favorite example to explain this form of one confining themselves to their senses happened this past May when I created a large-scale sound installation called *String Room*.

Four hundred feet of piano wire was strung up from the floor to ceiling and along the cement pillars of Co-Lab Projects, an art space in Austin, Texas.

The point of the piece was to give the city an instrument that visitors could interact with, first by me providing the participants with custom-made guitar picks to strum around the space, while also encouraging people to provide their own implements to instigate a new sonic relationship with the gallery.

The reviews for the installation were, pardon my pun, tone deaf.

The main complaint was that the strumming of the piece simply wasn't "loud enough." People felt it didn't work simply based on volume, which then rendered the installation useless.

The tone-deaf argument that the reviewers were unknowingly posing was questioning whether volume determined legitimacy within the framework of sound installation. If so, what does that mean of acoustic sounds that are not amplified? Is silence obsolete? If a sound is not sharp, up front, attention grabbing due to powered volume—does that make the piece a failure? How does one determine legitimacy of sound installations if they don't consider all volume levels?

"[F]or most people, hearing occurs all of the time, listening occurs most of the time and remains mysterious in its process.... "[L]istening remains a private matter for each of us." (Pauline Oliveros, Stony Brook Keynote speech, 2010)

This was one of many times that I wish Pauline was still around; I wish I could ask her opinions about it. But in a way I already know her answer: all sound is legitimate, it's the individual's ear that gets trained by society. But it's a private matter when it comes to how the ear is trained by each person. Hence the use of the word 'confine' for some.

One day, a young man came into the installation with a plastic cup that had a lot of condensation on its outside. The young man ran his fingers up and down one of the strings, which made a large, echoing warm tone, *à la* Ellen Fullman.

This change of sonic direction only proved to me that the piece did, in fact, work. If anything, it worked beautifully. I was simply the facilitator, offering one implement to play the piece. The CITY decided how it wanted to hear the piece simply by this young gentleman experimenting with the water on the wire. His individual perspective was not as confined as the reviewers because he was willing to experience through experimentation. Which was what the piece was made for, to encourage participants to interact with i t in order to expand their own experience within it.

Just like Pauline has said in the past, some hear all the time, but "the act of listening remains mysterious, private and unknown." I often forget, when discussing my concerns about hearing in contemporary times that I was taught to question this by Pauline. Our ears are being trained in all ways, with content and power. The role that we play as sound artists is to continue to introduce these sonic ideas that are outside of the mind of the general listener. By doing so we must also introduce and challenge our own ideas as well, since we as sound artists are not completely detached from this form of hearing/listening. The act of reminding each person to take a second to listen can be uncomfortable, due to our personal histories and experiences, but by asking oneself why they are uncomfortable, we could help break open a new way of listening. What a gift to be able to change an ear.

Anna Halprin

with

Phillip Greenlief,
Rashaun Mitchell,

Silas Riener,
Nina Martin,
and

Stephen Petronio

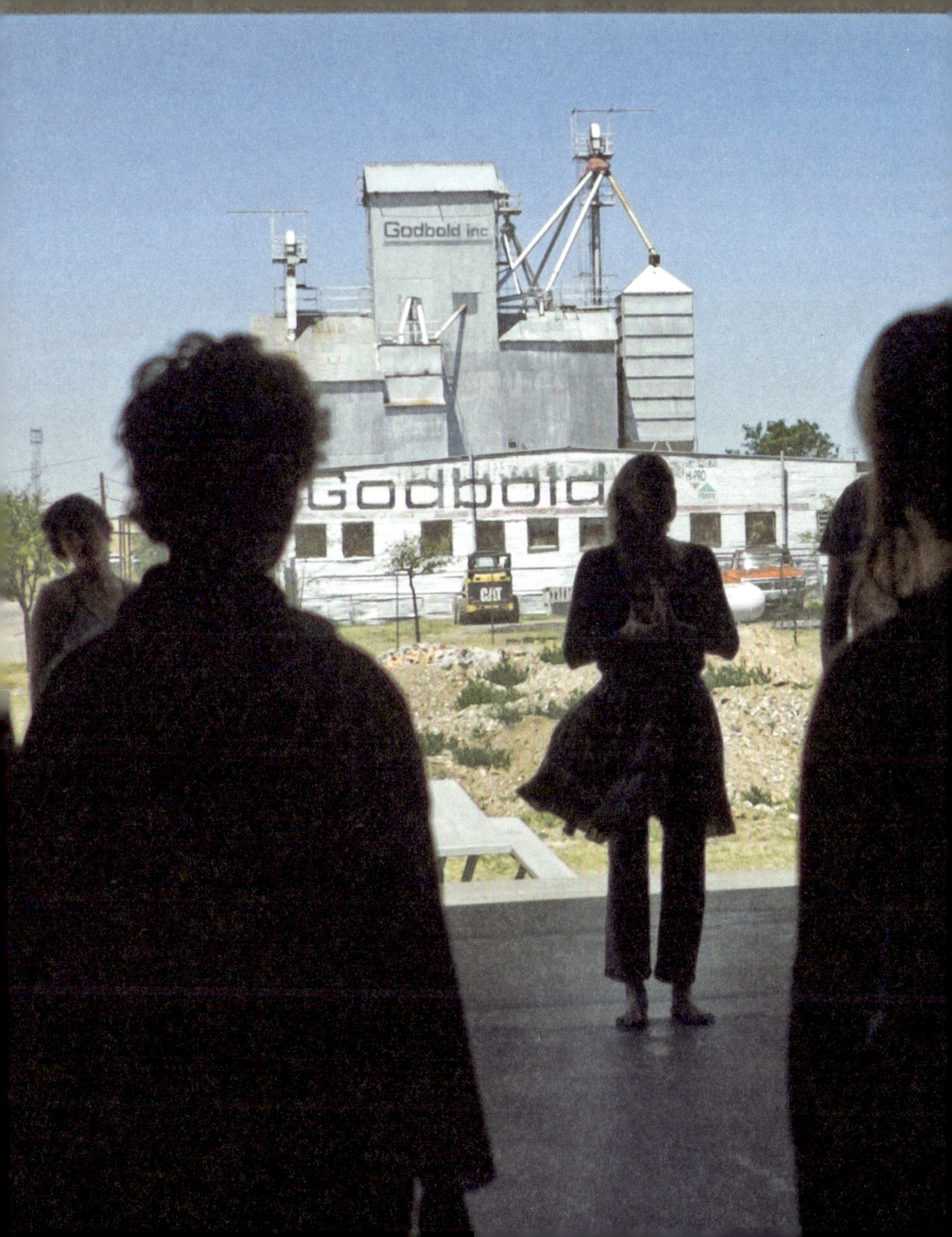
Godbold inc
Godbold
Hi-PRO
CAT

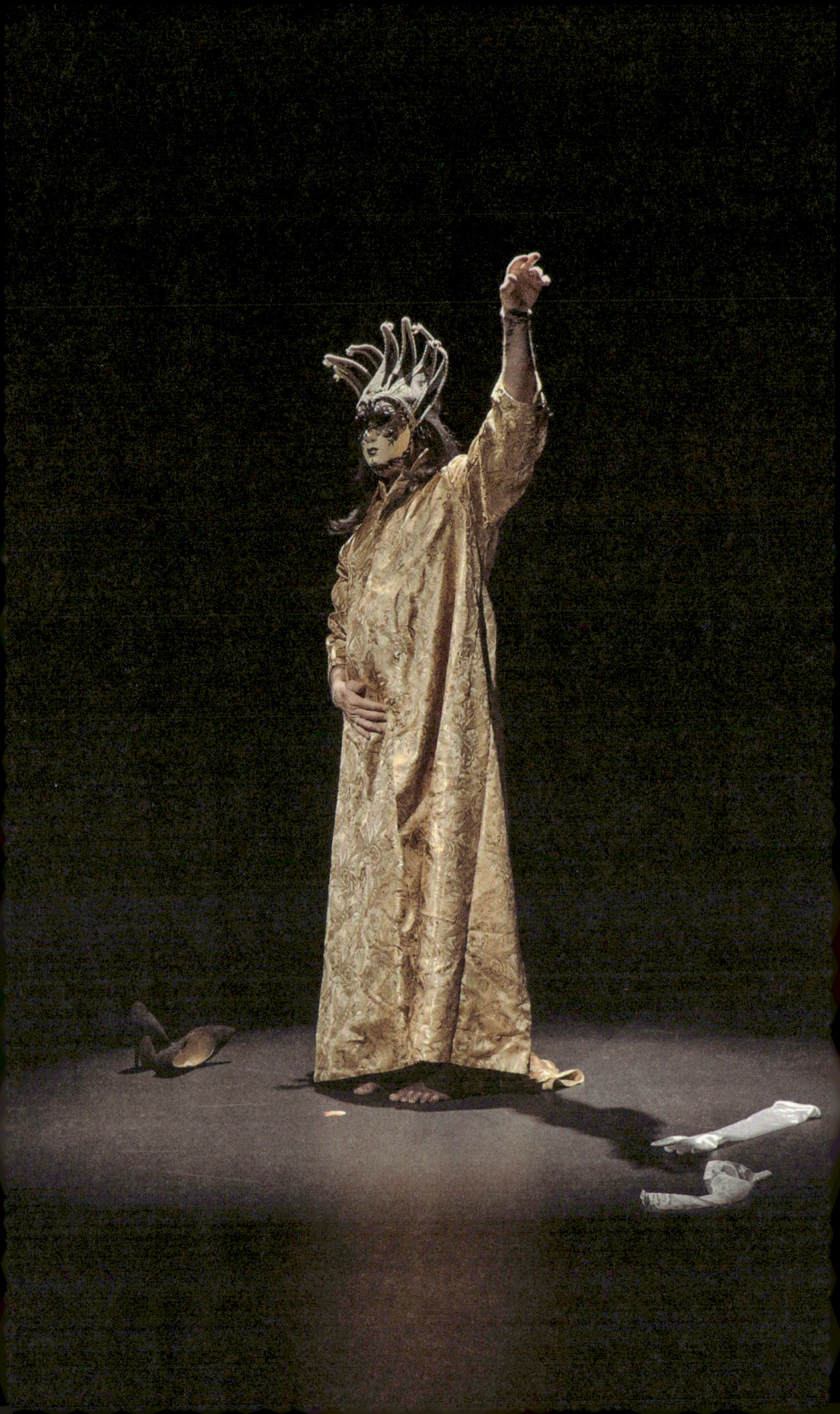

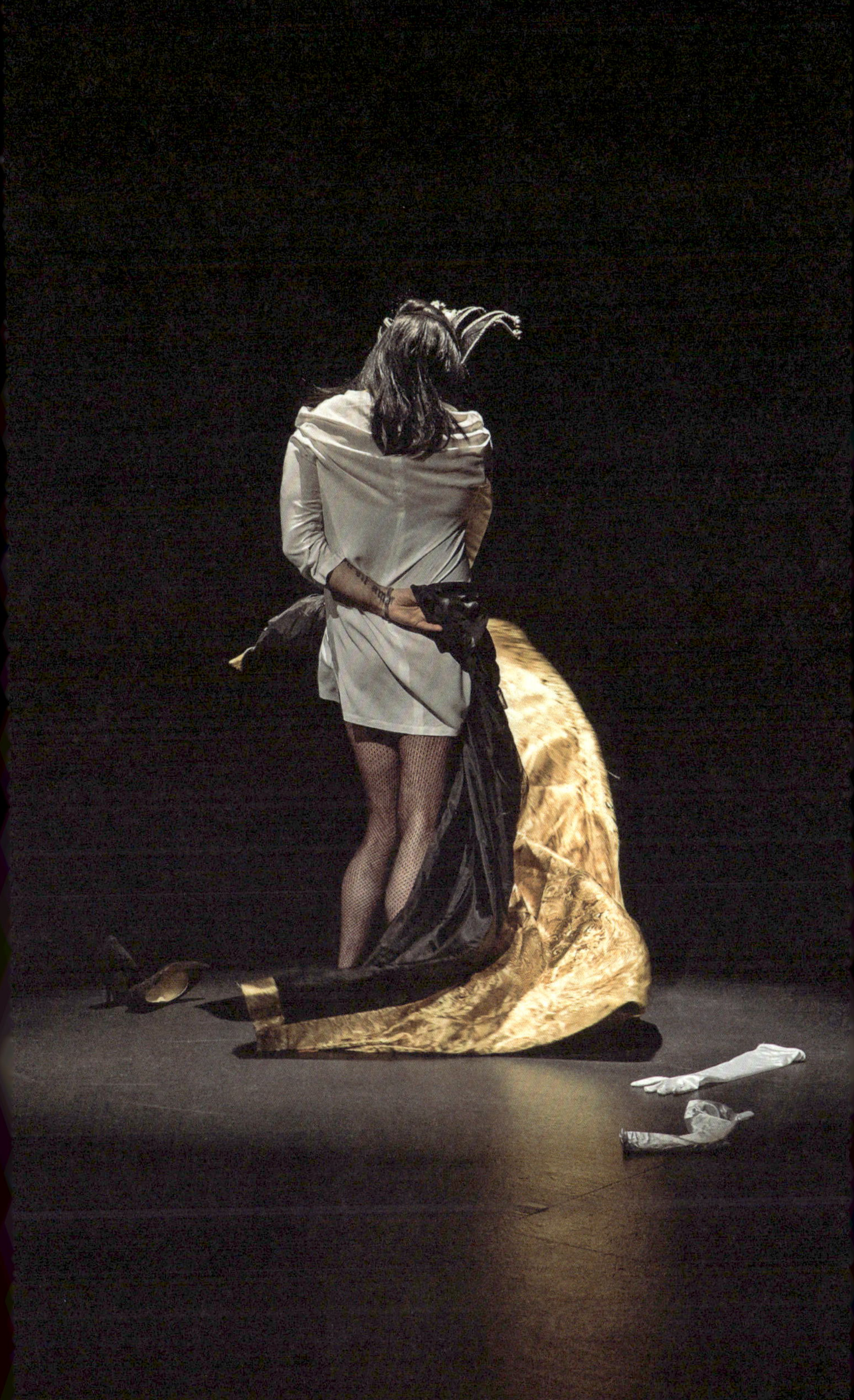

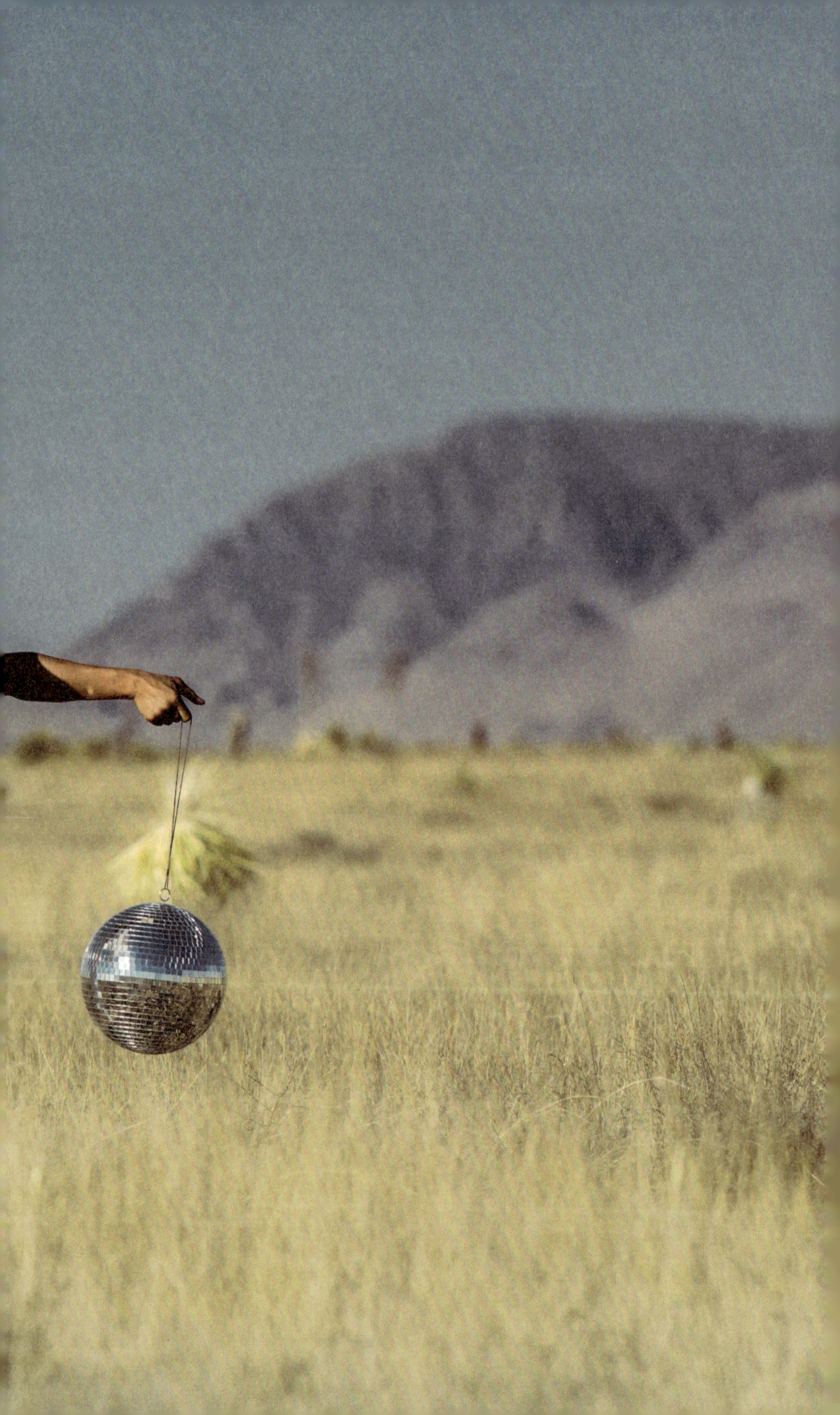

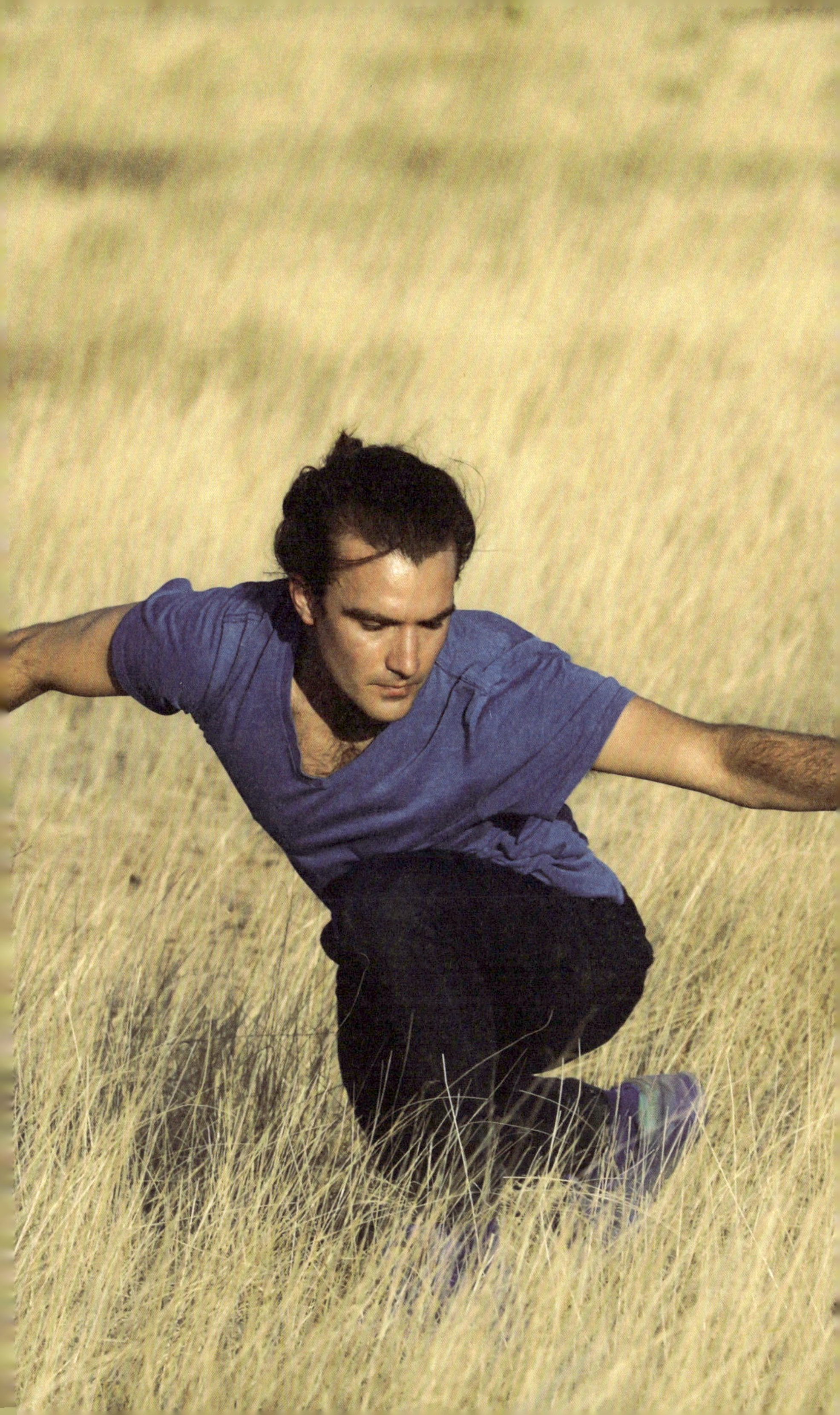

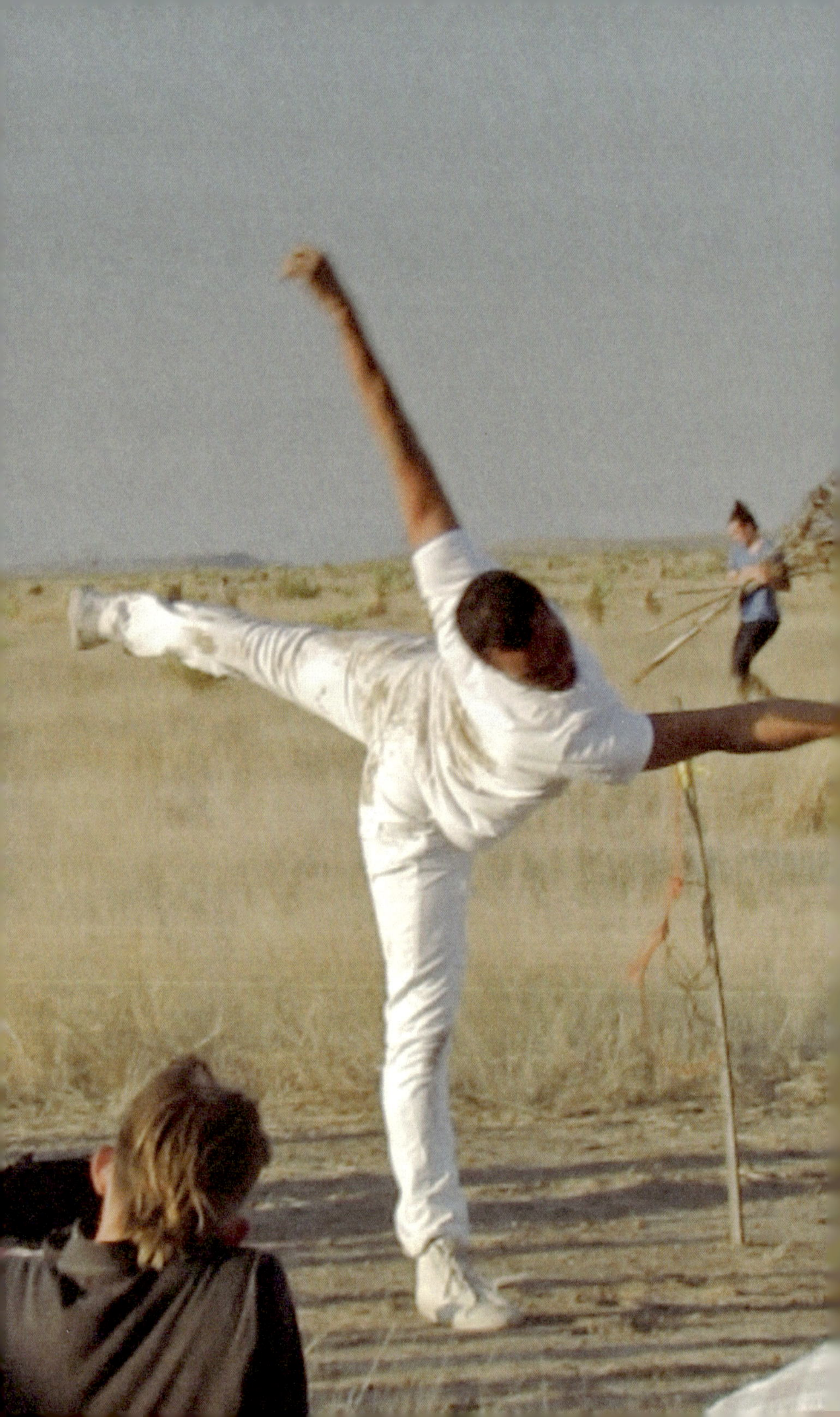

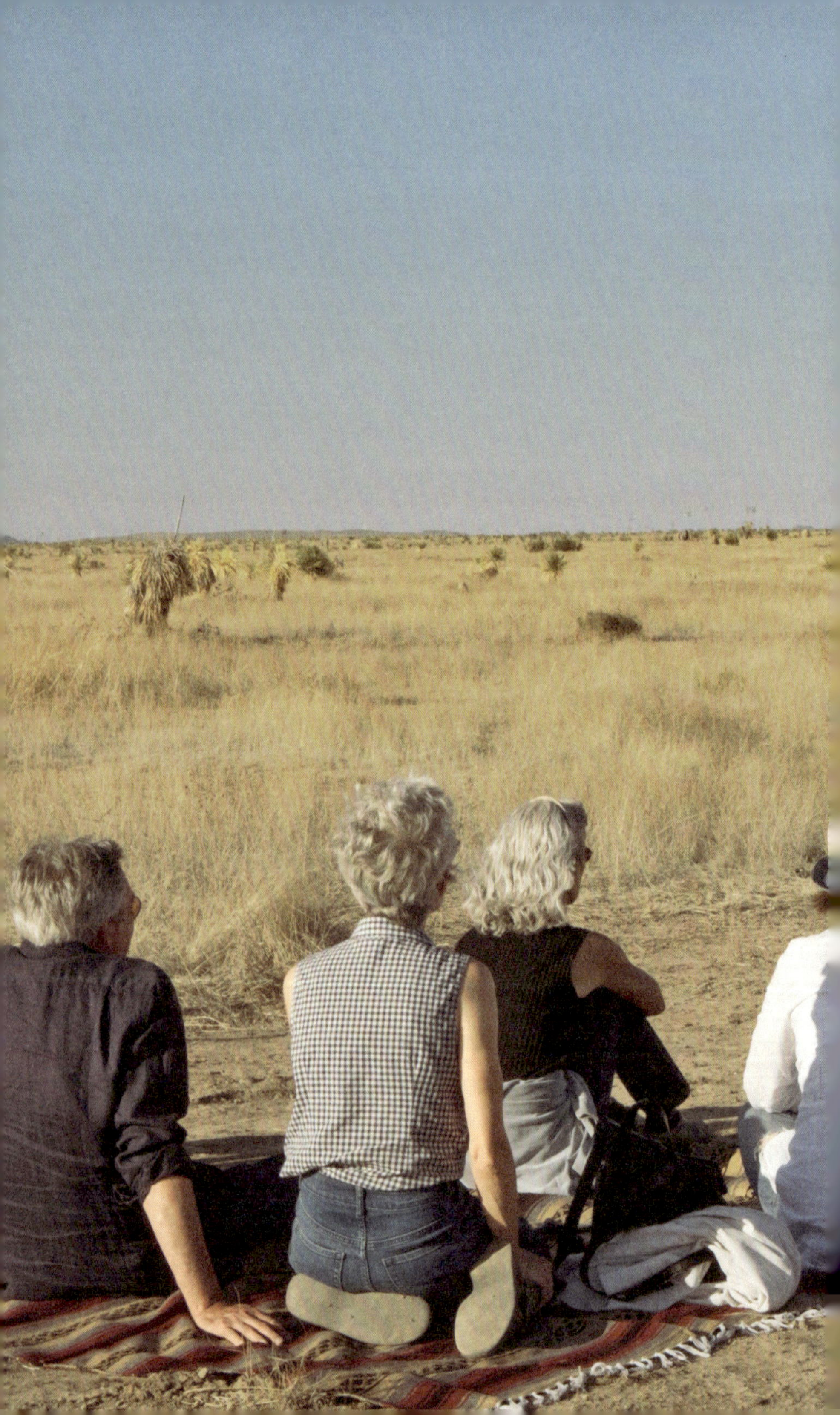

Anna Halprin,

Becoming Legible

in Marfa

Janice Ross

This is writing with a blindfold.

Seeing with memory dance events I did not witness live but respond to via saved impressions and images. So, I begin where *Marfa Sounding* in May 2017 ended.

I start with memory and move forward though the traces and remains of performance.

Being asked to respond to these 2017 *Marfa Sounding* performances past, focusing on Anna Halprin, is both daunting and liberating. Daunting because my impulse as a critic is to always try to hold the fleeting event in memory by intense viewing and yet these are events I did not experience in the live moment. Liberating because this option of reporting on a live event just witnessed is taken away at the start.

Write about what you did *not* see.

Write about what you did not see *in its moment* but which you have spent years watching, reflecting on, and creating prose about: Anna Halprin and her dance. Invert the formula of criticism by putting the dance in a room, shutting the door and inviting someone to write about what they glimpse through the keyhole or conjure from the sounds behind that door. This is a spirit reminiscent of the strategy of Robert Morris's *Box with the Sound of Its Own Making*. Doubly fitting then because this was a work he made shortly after taking a summer workshop with Anna on the dance deck where he experienced the radical concept for the time of process as dance. His box reimagines this as performance sculpture.

Write about what you did *not* see.

This is a challenge that fits well with the work of Anna Halprin because at the core of her aesthetic is a denial of the predictable, the customary, the routine.

My first thought is how curious are the ways Anna Halprin becomes fleetingly legible in the traces of *Marfa Sounding*. Juicy fragments: Claudia's poetic notebook entries, bits of Stephen's *The Courtesan and the Crone*, Silas and Rashaun's desert dance, a Vimeo collage of these performances all backgrounded by the 18th-century Adagio from Alessandro Marcello's Oboe Concerto in D Minor.

I am trying to imagine someone trying to imagine Anna's work. Her body. The body of her work. In the desert in Marfa.

Which Anna body is it they are reaching for? The one of her youth dancing Jewish-scented folk-dance forms in the mustard weed meadows of Woodside, California? There is a photo of her at her parents' redwood and glass home in Woodside, wearing an embroidered peasant top and skirt and dancing. Larry's Zionist influence hovers around her form like a mist as she pounds her heels and raises her arms upward.

Or is it another "Anna body" that *Marfa Sounding* invokes? Not a body of a specific space but the Aged Body that moved her through life, always finding, and telling, a truth about itself?

Meet the elusively coy body of *The Courtesan and the Crone.*

In this brief solo Anna played with representation itself in dance. She presented herself on the surface as a sensual young courtesan in a brocade cape and elaborate Commedia dell'arte mask her daughter Daria brought her from a trip to Venice. The rest is body affect and nuance as Anna constructs a plausible image of a youthful coquette. She then strips it away as she sheds her brocade cape and mask to reveal the withered body of her aged physical self, the crone. Anna's longtime fascination with the natural body found new ground in this questioning of: how does it age? After making *The Courtesan and the Crone* in 1999 she moved deeper into looking unflinchingly through dance at the aging female body.

Stephen's *Courtesan* takes us on a different journey, where not age but gender is the surprise the striptease discloses. His flirtation as the courtesan is a form of gender teasing while hers is temporal drag, a sampling of an old age that her resilience and energy into her 90s effectively precludes. The stripping back is the constant, the "Anna aesthetic" across both dances, both versions— her *Courtesan* and Stephen's. This hunt for who an individual is inside the dance has animated her work across her decades as a teacher, movement explorer, and instigator of contemporary movement rituals and dances.

Other bodies, other Anna bodies, come into view at *Marfa Sounding*:

The aged one of *Returning Home,* half buried in sand and mud, the piercing blue eyes blinking against the stillness of decaying bark

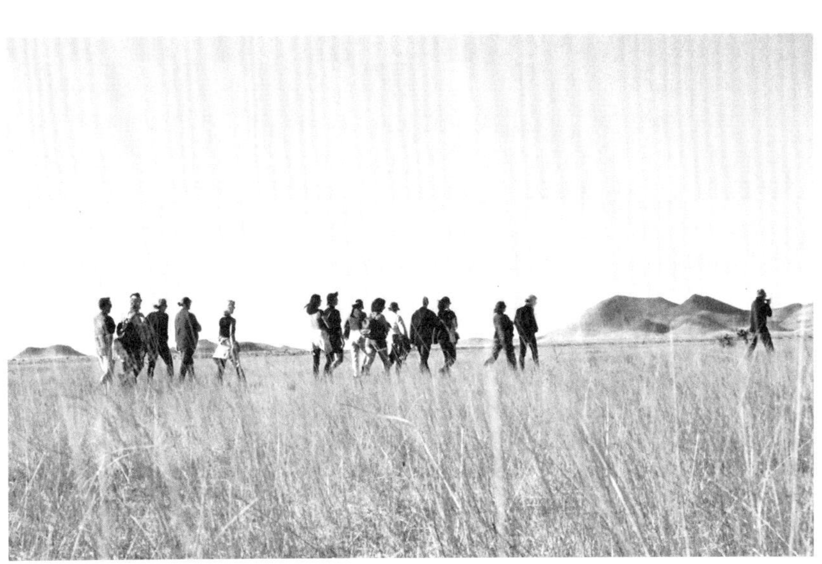

and moss. I see a glimmer of this in the red dust stains on Rashaun's bright white pants and shirt in the *Marfa Sounding* Vimeo. He is marked by his contact with the earth, suggesting his easy impact with the ground as a partner. Here is a clear stylistic legacy to Anna, her strategies for making work: She and her work taught us to *look off the stage and outside the studio and theatre*—that dance had strong and immediate links to the larger world—that it had important and distinctive insights to offer about that world. I have never been to Marfa but the setting looks stunning—a desert-scape that is tough in climate yet fragile in the small things that live there.

The frolicsome Anna is also evident in the whimsical way Silas and Rashaun gift members of the audience with spindly trees plucked from the distant desert (they look already dead, which is reassuring: that something that struggled so hard to live in these conditions has not been killed for the sake of a prop...). I think of the comic Anna from the 1940s James Broughton film, with her doing looney things on a bike, riding around San Francisco's Palace of Fine Arts with John Graham. No wait, that was later—the bike was in the late '50s? On a country road somewhere in Marin? And John Graham was in the '60s when she played a comical court dancer hiding among the massive columns of an outdoor faux Grecian temple.

What about other bodies set in motion by Anna over decades and decades of dancing, teaching dance, dance teaching? So many of these ripple through the *Marfa Sounding* documentation.

There is the body that always made one wonder, "How serious was the play and how playful was her seriousness?" During the 1960s and into the '70s there was a part of her that was in quiet dialogue with her more earnest colleagues working in that church on Washington Square on the other coast. Silas and Rashaun's dance suggests they come out of the post-post of that era when one of the strategies of both the aesthetic and politics of the time for Anna seems to have been to deliver work with a deliberate light-handedness—a casual ease—perhaps again in contrast to the modernist sternness?

What finally is repeatable in Anna's work that we might discover in the echoes of *Marfa Sounding* here? Is it the dance or

is it the dance as a catalyst for conversations that cluster around
their own immediate pressing concerns of the moment in which
they are performed?

Anna's voice will be the most resonant here—a final rhetorical
sound to the Soundings:

"It's always been part of my art process to start a process and
bring it to a point of completion—just as a performance is one kind
of completion. I start a class by saying, 'Let's divide the class in half.
Half of you are witnesses, and the other half—let's see what you've
done with this material.' When you use a creative process, you
bring it to some kind of fruition. There needs to be some
integration, some sense of, 'Well, what was this really all about?
What kind of experience did I have? How is it going to affect my life
or anybody else's life? What did it mean to me to do this? What did
it mean to you?' So, for me that has always been a way of
continuing with an art process."

Ending with Meaning

Andrew Abrahams
in conversation

with

Cate Cole Schrim

In 2017, *Marfa Sounding* focused on Anna Halprin's impact on successive generations of artists, dancers, and choreographers. This question of influence is often made manifest at the intersection of pedagogy and film: encountering her work either through in-person workshops and communal experiences of embodied learning or through flickering images on a screen. As part of *Marfa Sounding*, Abrahams's experimental documentary *Anna Halprin–Embracing Earth* (1995, 23 minutes) was shown in the context of a screening program devoted to cinema's engagement with the choreographer's practice. This series also included two films by Jacqueline Caux: *Anna Halprin–Who Says I Have to Dance in a Theater* (2006, 50 minutes) and *Anna Halprin–Out of Boundaries* (2004, 53 minutes).

CATE COLE SCHRIM   At what point in your life did you begin working with Anna?

ANDREW ABRAHAMS   I met Anna because I was interested in improv dance and the kind of work she was doing in using dance in a more unstructured way. I was living in Los Angeles at the time and going to grad school for visual anthropology. A friend told me about her work up in San Francisco. She was working with the HIV community. In particular, she was using dance as a way to address the AIDS epidemic. I thought that sounded really interesting, especially because of my background in anthropology and in looking at ritual and performance in that context. So, I went up to San Francisco and I met her. I was in her workshop, and I just really connected to the work that she was doing. Eventually, probably about a year later, I moved up to the Bay Area and I did my Master's thesis on Anna's work with people living with HIV. I got involved in filming the group she was working with over a period of time, and that resulted in a film I made called *Positive Motion* (1991, 37 minutes). Also, my Master's thesis, which was entitled "Ritual, Reflexivity and Healing in a Dance by Men Challenging AIDS," looked at her work from an anthropological perspective.

CCS   How did Anna encourage those living with HIV to connect emotional content to physical expression?

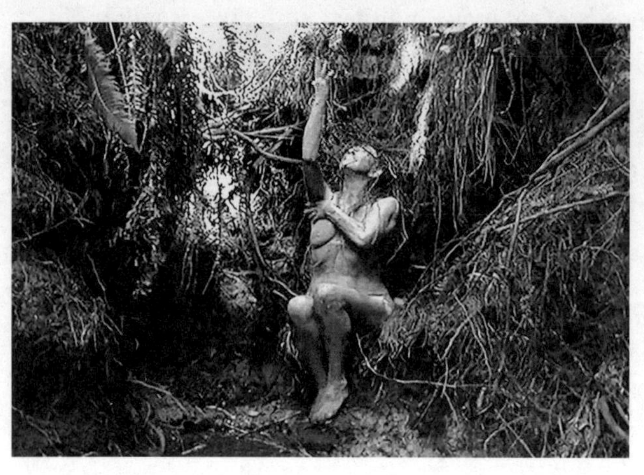

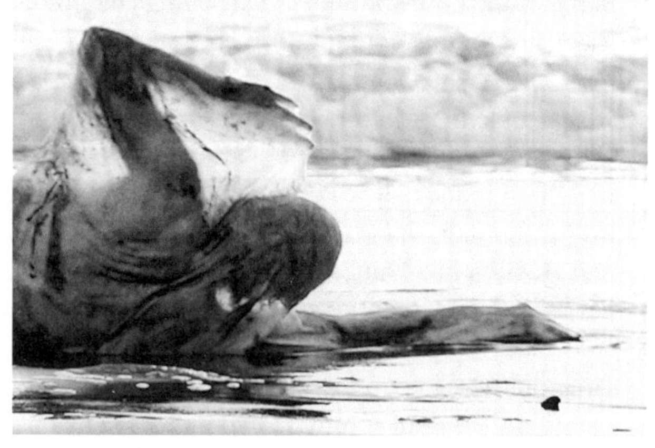

AA   Anna was encouraging a connection between what you're
doing and the way that you're feeling. There was a certain
emphasis on transparency of the movement. The word she
would use is "authenticity." So that what you're expressing in
movement is what you're feeling. I think that is really
important to all of us, but it is especially important to people
with life-threatening illnesses and to those who have become
disconnected from their bodies, or for those whose body
has become, in some way, an enemy. So that alone is healing,
to find a way of being connected to the body.

CCS   As exemplified by the Planetary Dance, Anna sees dance not
just as a healing force but also as a community-based
practice. Do you see the opportunity for healing as being
more impactful as a group process?

AA   That's an interesting question: the issue of personal versus
communal healing. I think it works on both levels. I think that
one of the points that Anna tries to stress is that there really
is no difference. We are embedded in community. When we're
healing the self, we're also healing the greater self, whether
that self is the environment (and often it's because she's very
interested in the natural environment), but also the greater
Self—meaning our relation to society. I do believe there's
a connection. Her work with the HIV community was exactly
that: At the same time that the participants were healing
themselves, they were also healing the group. The group was
essential to the self-healing. In looking at it from a ritualistic
sense, there is a bond between the performer (the individual)
and the witnesses (the people who are watching). And when
I say "performing," I do not mean—and Anna does not mean—
in the sense of entertainment or remembering lines. Rather,
performance is embodying your role or your work in the ritual.

      That's something that I've taken with me in my work as
a filmmaker: the sacredness of the fact that I'm not penetrating
someone else's experience or imposing my own experience. I
look at the camera as a witness who's receiving the experience
or "performance" of the subject. It's empowering for the

101

subject. At the same time, it's humbling for the viewer or, in my case, the "filmer." That idea—which is so important to me—was profoundly influenced by my work with Anna. In terms of filmmaking, you have the subject that's being witnessed by the filmmaker and then the larger witness, which are the viewers of the film. It ripples out from personal to the collective.

ccs In *Returning Home*, Anna holds reverence for physical space in the form of nature, but also, especially, the physical body. As such, can you speak to how aging, illness, or other ailments can inform dance as an artistic process, given the body and its limits?

AA I think what Anna is doing is making deep connections between the human body and the natural body, embedding us deeply in the context of nature, looking at the human being and the human body as nature. If you do that, you don't judge the body. You look at the body the same way you would look at a tree that changes over time, or erosion, or fire in the landscape. I think that's essential to the way Anna looks at the body, and her work in general. If you take out that judgmental aspect, it's just the body being itself. In the same way that we look at nature as being beautiful in all its many forms, we can also look at the body in that way.

ccs In your essay "Breaking the Box: Dancing the Camera with Anna Halprin," which was published in the book *Envisioning Dance on Film and Video* (Routledge, 2003), you imply that the act of capturing Anna working with others was, in effect, an extension of the choreography. Can you explain how filmmaking led to you partaking in the movement you were capturing?

AA I think it starts with what Anna teaches, which is about being in the body, being authentic in the body, being aware of the sensations in the body, and being aware of the relationship to what's outside the body as well. It's awareness inside and outside, and the understanding that we are always in relationship. I think that's a really important aspect of Anna's work. You're always working with elements in nature, and connecting them to your own nature. If I'm doing that as a filmmaker, I'm using my camera to connect. So the camera is my instrument in the same way that Anna talks about the body as being her instrument. Of course, the body is also my instrument, but creatively I have the added instrument of the camera, with which I'm connecting to my subjects or to the world around me. That's how it becomes a dance. Especially when I was filming dance, I became part of the dance. I would actually move my body in relationship with the dance and the dancers. In that way, you can also lose the sense of boundary between self and other. That is the artistic moment: art meaning to link or to connect. As Anna would say, that's where the art comes in, when you're making an association between self and other, between what's going on inside the experience and its expression.

CCS   Have you been able to implicate Anna's ideologies in your own pedagogy?

AA   I teach a workshop at Esalen which very much started with concepts drawn from Anna's *oeuvre*. It's called "Intimacy and Exposure: The Alchemy of Photography." I'm using the photographic camera to explore some of the themes we've discussed: to explore the natural world in similar ways that Anna might use the body. I encourage students to look at the different aspects or relationships inherent in photography, all of which interact and interrelate. There's the descriptive level of what the photo *is*, and then there's the emotional or affective level, as well as the associative level: what the photo conjures or recalls. Anna works on these levels in her teachings as a way of finding meaning in the dance, and I think I've adopted these principles from her.

CCS   In working with Anna throughout all these years, which of her ideologies have been the most formative for you as an artist?

103

AA   I think all of what we've talked about today is important. We talked about the relationship between the performer and the witness and, in my case, between the subject and the filmmaker. That relationship of how one supports the other, and how the very act of witnessing becomes a really important part of healing, enables me to look at what I do as a form of healing. I don't think too many people do that in my field. And I don't just think of healing in terms of how my films will help people, but how the process itself is healing. And that comes from working with Anna. Also the idea that art informs life. Anna inverts the saying that life informs art. She is firmly entrenched in the way that art can reveal something important about our own lives. Using this artistic process, we can learn about ourselves. For Anna—and myself—art doesn't have much meaning apart from that.

I think *that's* the great legacy of Anna ... that she's not just creating art for art's sake. It's not just a concept. She doesn't start with an idea that is then illustrated in the art or in the dance. She starts with authenticity of movement—fully embodying the self and, going from there, she asks, "What is the body saying?" It is then that you start understanding the meaning that art has for your life. We don't start with the meaning; we end with the meaning. That has been especially instructive for me in looking at my own artistic creations: What does my art tell me about my life? How does it make connections between inside and outside? How has it made me more whole? What possibilities does it have to heal others?

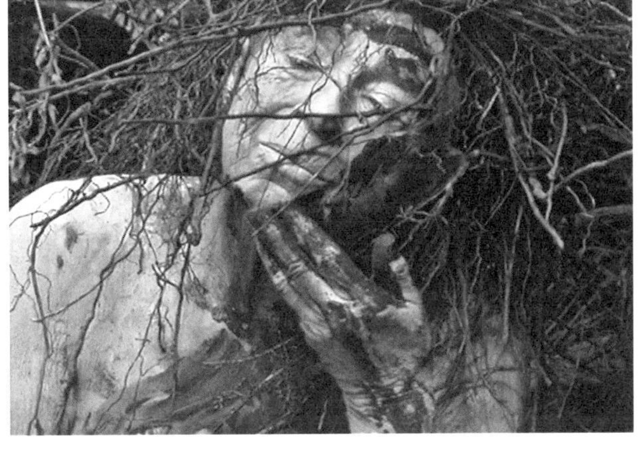

The Body

Wants

Wendy Vogel

How does the body register the space between places? This question is a preoccupation of both choreography and minimalist art. The experience of some distances exceeds their measurement, like the 2000-mile trip from Brooklyn to Marfa, Texas. Three weeks ago, I traveled to the tiny West Texas town (population: 1,981) for *Marfa Sounding*, a three-day program (May 26–28) honoring the Northern California-based choreographer Anna Halprin. The journey took me around 14 hours: two New York subway lines, a New Jersey Transit train, two flights, and a 200-mile drive. But the full enormity of the distance didn't strike me until my flight's final descent into El Paso. Roused from a catnap in my window seat, I snapped open the hot shade to reveal gently gridded desert as far as I could see. A few minutes later, sparse shrubs and low-lying buildings zoomed into view. After landing, I jumped in my rental car and set off, amid the hardness of the Chihuahuan desert landscape's flat-topped mountains and arid expanses. Although Marfa's outsize presence in the art world has been crafted by Donald Judd, this feeling of venturing to the edge where nature and culture meet felt in line with Halprin's work of translating personal sensation to movement.

Marfa Sounding 2017 was the second of three yearly festivals devoted to performance practitioners whose work intersects with (and complicates) the history of minimalism. Marfa is home to more than a dozen permanent minimalist installations commissioned through Donald Judd's Chinati Foundation. Known since the 1960s for his "specific objects" of serially produced geometric elements, Judd purchased a tract of land in 1979 in Marfa—a town near the Mexican border with a railroad stop and a handful of former military buildings. Judd and his artist friends, including Dan Flavin and John Chamberlain, created site-specific works for Marfa's architecture and landscape. Curated by Jennifer Burris, *Marfa Sounding* brought Halprin's choreographic practice into conversation with Judd's art. Rather than simply presenting her work, the five events comprising *Marfa Sounding* included screenings, a movement class, an interpretation of one of her works by the New York–based choreographer Stephen Petronio, and a commissioned performance by dancers Rashaun Mitchell and Silas

Riener (with Phillip Greenlief). *Marfa Sounding* framed Halprin's importance through a transmission of her ideas, across bodies, generations, time and space.

Halprin—now 96 years old—continues to inspire through her legacy and ongoing work (though unable to attend *Marfa Sounding*, on June 4th, she hosted her thirty-sixth annual Planetary Dance for peace on, and with, the Earth at California's Mt. Tamalpais State Park.) Beginning in the 1960s, her exploration of task-based and everyday motion laid the foundation for postmodern dance. She moved to Marin County, California after World War II, where her husband, the landscape architect Lawrence Halprin, constructed an outdoor deck attached to their home as a dance space framed by the forest just outside. There, Halprin started teaching dancers like Trisha Brown, Simone Forti, and Yvonne Rainer, as well as artists like John Cage and later, Carrie Mae Weems. Her company, the San Francisco Dancers Workshop, moved dance out of the proscenium theater, from city streets to airplane hangars. While some of Halprin's students went on to form the Judson Dance Theater in 1962 and work with score-based performance in New York, Halprin remained on the West Coast, creating work addressing such themes as racial injustice, environmental degradation, AIDS, and aging. Her teaching practice has received as much recognition, if not more, than her own work. She was thus a fitting choice for *Marfa Sounding*, which was co-presented by the pedagogical organization Fieldwork Marfa (a collaboration between Beaux-Arts Nantes Saint-Nazaire and HEAD–Genève) and the performance organization Marfa Live Arts.

There's an element of transgression in bringing Halprin's work—ephemeral, collaborative, and engaged with questions of social justice—into a town dominated by the permanent installations at Chinati. These works uphold values of abstraction and timelessness as much as they deny certain aspects of the diversity of human experience (for instance, Roni Horn is the only woman represented in the Chinati holdings). Still, there are ties that bind Halprin's practice to Judd's. Like Judd, Halprin rejected the narrative grandiosity of modernism, epitomized in dance by such performers as Martha Graham. Both artists also adhere to site-specificity and took value in cultivating spaces that might inspire the creativity of other artists.

In Jacqueline Caux's 2006 documentary on Halprin, *Who Says I Have to Dance in a Theater?*, Halprin details how she arrived at her somatic vocabulary. Trained in kinesiology as well as dance, she creates feedback between emotions and movement, considering "how that material could be shaped artistically." In the 1960s, her dancers often performed ordinary movements in the nude (as in the score-based work *Parades and Changes*, 1965–67); following her 1969 performance *Ceremony of Us*, working with black and white dancers to process the racial divide following the Watts riots, her work of the 1970s and '80s engaged populations such as cancer and AIDS patients. In her 80s, she addressed such questions as "How can I die gracefully?" and "What's the legacy I want to leave behind?" This documentary includes clips from works such as *Embracing Earth* (Andrew Abrahams's 1995 film of dancers on Halprin's property, slowly moving through the woods or suspended from trees in amniotic-looking mesh), and *Intensive Care* (a dance from 2000 about illness and death). One of the several documentaries screened in Marfa, the film was projected in Building 98, an adobe structure that once served as Army bachelor officers' quarters and a home for World War II–era German prisoners of war. Today the building is the headquarters of the International Women's Association devoted to art and healthy aging.

Halprin's ideas were shown and also enacted. At the community space the Crowley Theater, dancer Nina Martin held a morning workshop based on the tenets of Halprin's practice: that movement can be a way to relate to one's environment. A Marfa resident, Martin has created postmodern dance and experimental theater since the 1970s. "I am the body, and the body wants," Martin said, as she introduced the participants (myself included) to two movement exercises. For several minutes, we writhed intuitively on the stage like fussy babies, redirecting our movements to avoid choreographic completion. For the "sibling dance," Martin threw open the stage's back door. Sunlight and dry heat flooded the black box, erasing the illusion of an imaginary theatrical space. We chose partners and pushed each other, back to back; rather than

traditional mirroring exercises of improvisation, we challenged
ourselves on the level of weight and balance.

Later that evening, Stephen Petronio (a longtime friend of
Martin's) embodied Halprin's spirit, dancing *The Courtesan and the
Crone* (1999). Lit from behind, Petronio approached the audience,
moving downstage in a cape and mask. He executed dramatic,
angular gestures of seduction: beckoning with his hands, then
revealing fishnet stockings and red bikini briefs under his golden
cape. At the conclusion of the performance, he stripped to a white
slip. Horrified with his elderly appearance, he looked to the sky,
hands clasped to his face, before crumpling to the ground. Later, in
a conversation with Martin and curator Jennifer Burris following
the performance, Petronio explained that Halprin had selected the
score-based dance for him to perform after he visited her in
California. He has since performed it at the Fabric Workshop and
Museum in Philadelphia (as part of a collaboration with Halprin
and artist Janine Antoni) and in the multipart series *Bloodlines*
at the Joyce Theater, a kind of "autobiography through dance," in
which his company stages historical works that shaped his artistic
development. The program has also included works by artists like
Yvonne Rainer and Trisha Brown, who hired Petronio as the first
male dancer in her company in 1979. Since the 1980s, Petronio
has developed his own work on themes such as gay sexuality, the
AIDS crisis, and aggression, abandoning the anti-spectacular
doctrines of the Judson Theater. In Petronio's interpretation, the
message of *The Courtesan and the Crone*—that sexuality can function
as a site of both power and loss—becomes radically reconfigured.

The weekend concluded with a new improvisational work by
Rashaun Mitchell and Silas Riener, accompanied by experimental
musician Phillip Greenlief. Formerly dancers for Merce
Cunningham—a friend of Halprin's—Mitchell and Riener have
collaborated since 2010. A generation removed from Petronio, they
carry on a legacy informed both by '90s body politics and '70s
dance. Their improvisational performance, roughly structured in
three movements, took place just outside Marfa, on 20 acres of
land purchased by Fieldwork Marfa for art studios and housing for
resident artists and students. Based on Claude Bragdon's

110

architecture in harmony with nature, Mitchell and Riener's sunset performance included movements based on animals (jumping like jackrabbits), extensions, contact improvisation, and voguing. Greenlief moved with them through the field, blowing lightly through his saxophone reed, the majority of sound coming from his fingers on the keys. In the work's final minutes, Mitchell performed with a disco ball, swinging it like a low pendulum and then holding it tightly between his legs: the clock, sex, birth. Riener passed yucca branches to members of the audience, recalling a scene from Anna Halprin's performance of *Still Dance*, and bringing us into dialogue with the dancers and the field. This unity between performers and audience honored Halprin's ethos.

After leaving Marfa, I spent a few days in Miami, trying to reconcile my time in the bleached-out desert among tropical vegetation, brilliant skies, and unrelenting humidity. There, I binge-watched *I Love Dick*, Jill Soloway's TV adaptation of Chris Kraus's 1997 epistolary novel-as-feminist-theory. Transposed to Marfa (the book is set in LA, among other places), the series played upon the town's cinematic cowboy image. Love-interest Dick—evidently modeled on the stereotype of a minimalist artist—was manly and dismissive; narrator Chris—an avatar for Kraus—was a tortured woman hysterical with desire. The feminism of Soloway's show was not always triumphant, and the depiction of Marfa is reductive, but the final scene held some promise. Chris walks into the desert, failed but defiant, menstrual blood dripping down her leg. Her fluids marked the space between her body and the land, much like Halprin's dancers sought communion with the nature that surrounded them. I pondered whether Soloway knew Halprin's work, but decided it didn't matter: either way, her message carried through, of movement as performance, of performance as political.

Marfa Notebook

Claudia La Rocco

I see Rashaun's body being tossed as if by an invisible wave; how amazing, I think, the things he can do.

Later he tells me that was the wind, that he was trying desperately to keep his footing, that falling was scary and painful. This information will be seconded by Silas. Phillip's nasal passages and lungs and really his whole body will be wrecked for days: what it is to circular breathe in the desert.

They take us on a morning site visit, explaining that the wind is easier then. "This is hard: I do like it when there is something in the landscape to address," R. says. The eye wants structure. S. finds a rattlesnake skin. He and R. discuss. P. walks out into the distance. There is the sound of crickets, mostly the sound of wind. There are barely-there paths beaten into the dust, which is the color and consistency of nutmeg powder. A jackrabbit rushes.

The rumpled mountain spines in the distance. Grit in everyone's teeth. A dog who is no one's dog shows up, hangs around; P. points, smiles, says *Stalker*, referring to the Tarkovsky movie. The dog that just showed up. Scraps of metal and the dully colorful box cars of a long train.

Writing this now, months later, I think of something said to me by a filmmaker who has for many years had a day job that involves shooting the studio practice of performing artists: how it has diminished the idea of the "finished product" as the actual thing, knowing there are so many hours and days and months surrounding that moment in time when the curtain parts.

Of course, there is no curtain here. There is very little to stop the tumbleweeds. The restaurants run out of food. "I was almost unable to think while we were out there," S. says, later that day, while the others nap and he and I sit on the poured concrete deck, talking about this and that.

I see him running with rapid, elegant direction shifts, legacy of his soccer years. Further in the distance, R. standing still, holding a white sail of fabric. P. working a midrange frequency on his mouthpiece.

The night before they had talked about what would disappear, what wouldn't. Who held this land originally, who owns it now. "It's always been about land, who can afford to access and control the land, or the water, or the electricity."

At one point in the performance, R. walks so far into the distance, I forget to look for him. He is another part of this big landscape. I think of something he said that night before, after we had flown from various points, met in the El Paso airport, stumbled upon fantastic Mexican food and taken the long, dark drive to this strange art colony, all of us with tired bodies and excited minds, all of us sprawled in a stranger's vacant bungalow, the project still an idea more than an actuality: "There is that lure of doing something impressive."

When you disappear, you gesture toward the land.

We (the watchers) are all on blankets, or standing, or clumped in small groups being art world people. There is the ubiquitous medium of the smart phone, dully glowing rectangles held up here and there like miniature recording lanterns. A way to sidestep the present for the perfect future.

S. catches his hands behind his back and hinges his torso, stalking across our field of vision in big, geometric lines. R. makes a voluptuous turn until the wind catches up to him and spirals him down into the dirt and brush, where he stays, crawling slowly now, moving almost not at all. P. pushes his breath through circular loops, wanders an uneven line on the perimeter.

All day there had been a leisurely conversation about outfits, props, positioning. I couldn't see the point of the disco ball. Lack of imagination. Can't see it, until there R. is, swinging the ball on its cord as he stalks through the tawny, almost-iridescent vegetation: the beauty and right-wrongness of that object, the lights of it hitting P.'s saxophone as he moves through various fingerings. S.'s turn now to be a barely-there body in the distance, running and running and running. Why it's important to insert what doesn't belong, what can be political about that; S. quietly, insistently linking such insertions to a submerged queer identity.

I think about how many hours I have spent with these three individuals. How much I love them.

"Anna Halprin talks about, it's a body in an environment, it's not a representation of something else. So, what can a body do, what does a body want to do."

There are horses running in the distance. Agitated, aware of us, and then still.

Sometimes the notes are close together, sometimes far apart.

It's easy for a body to get swallowed up.

Deep sideways lunge. Gloved fingertips to toe. Foot up. Sideways balance. Multiphonics whistling into and against the air.

Tarek Atoui

with

Amma Ateria,
Jad Atoui,

and

Robert Aiki
Aubrey Lowe

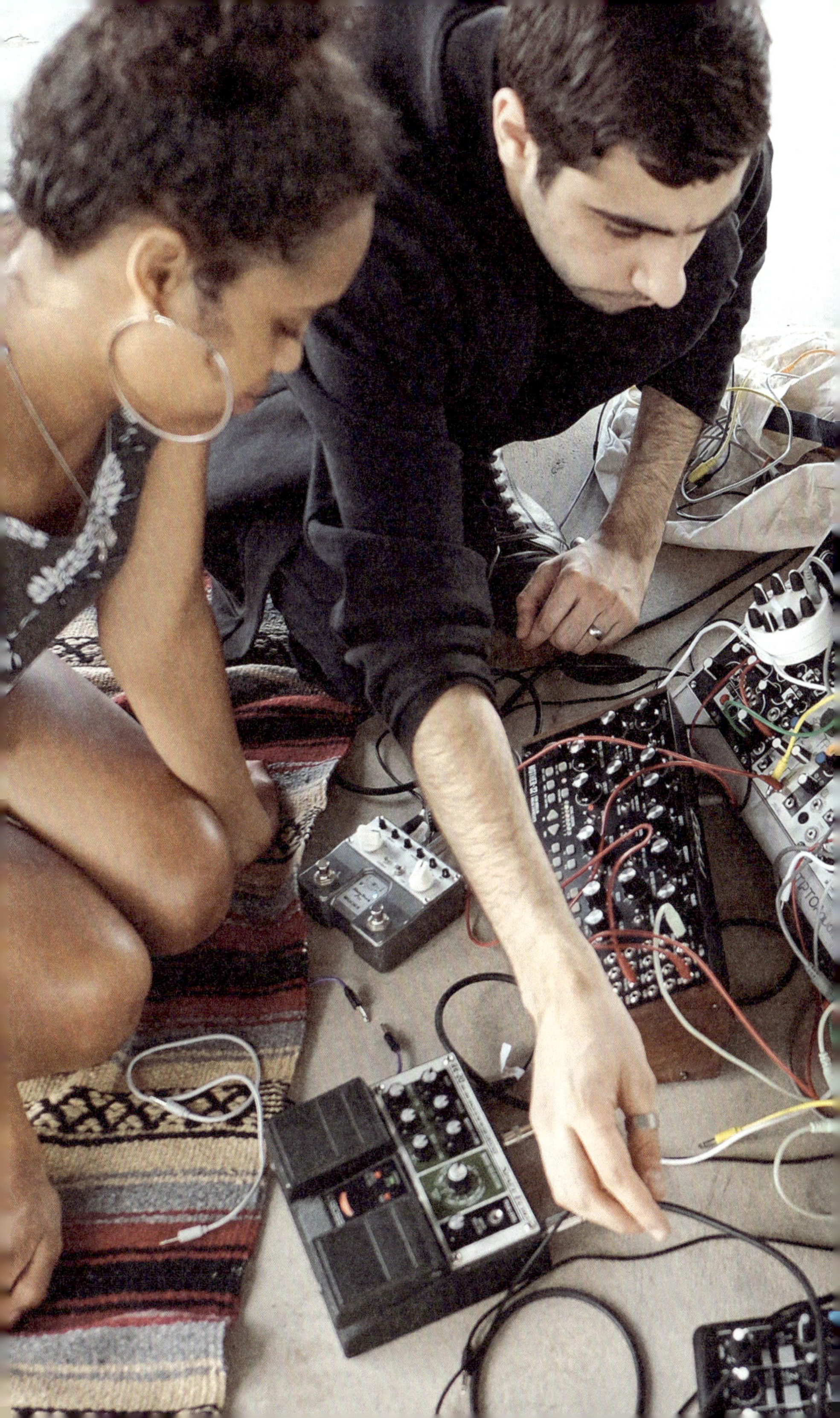

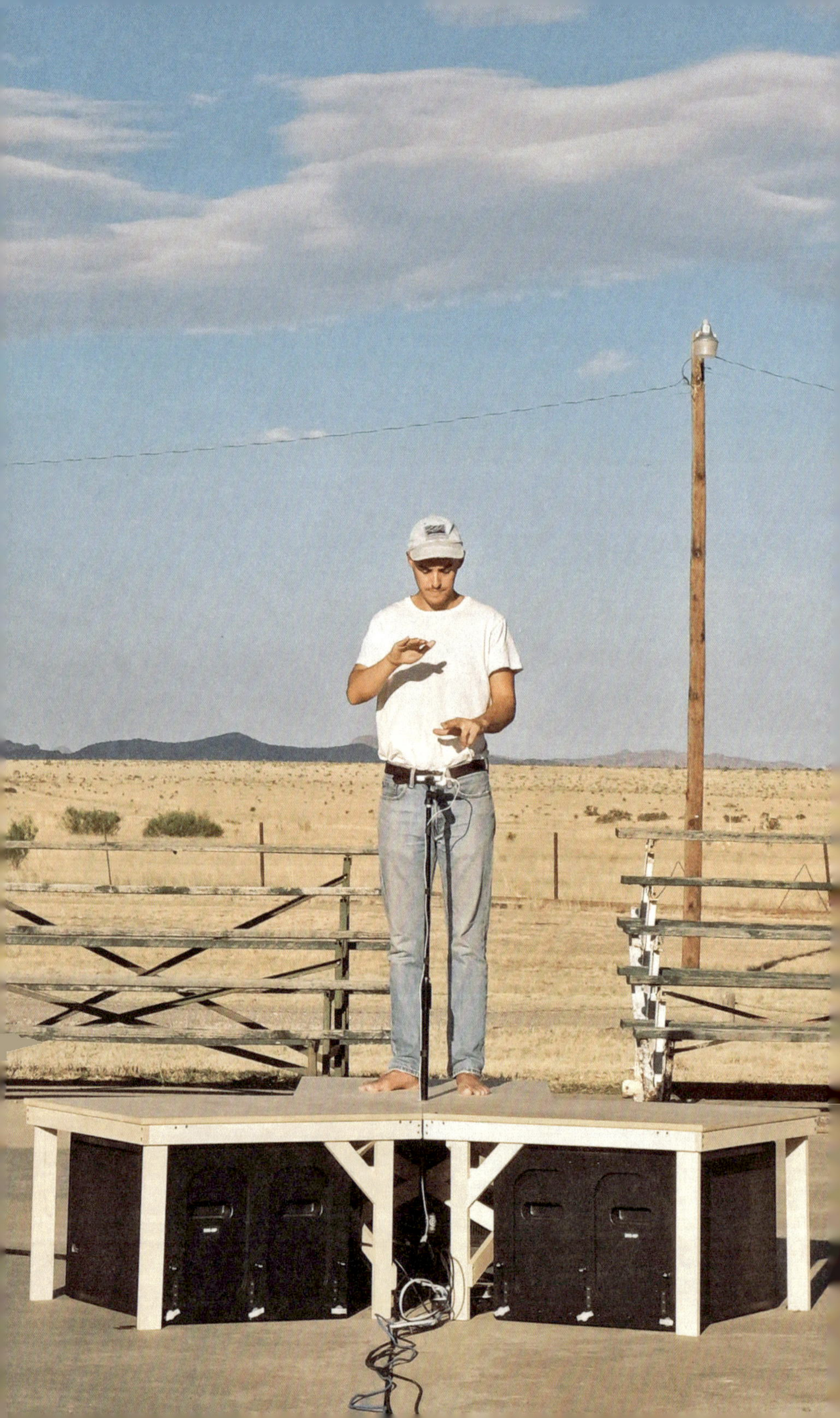

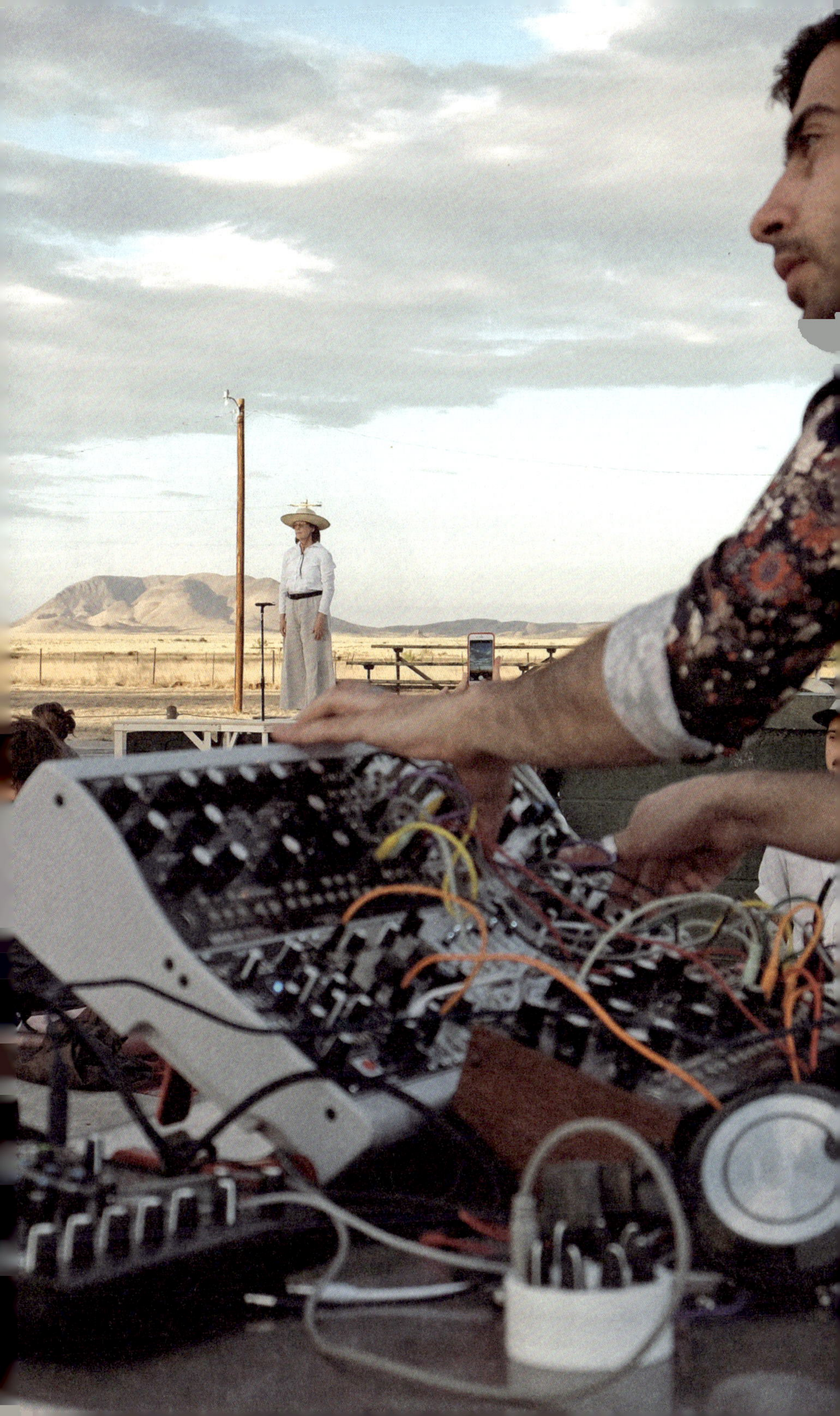

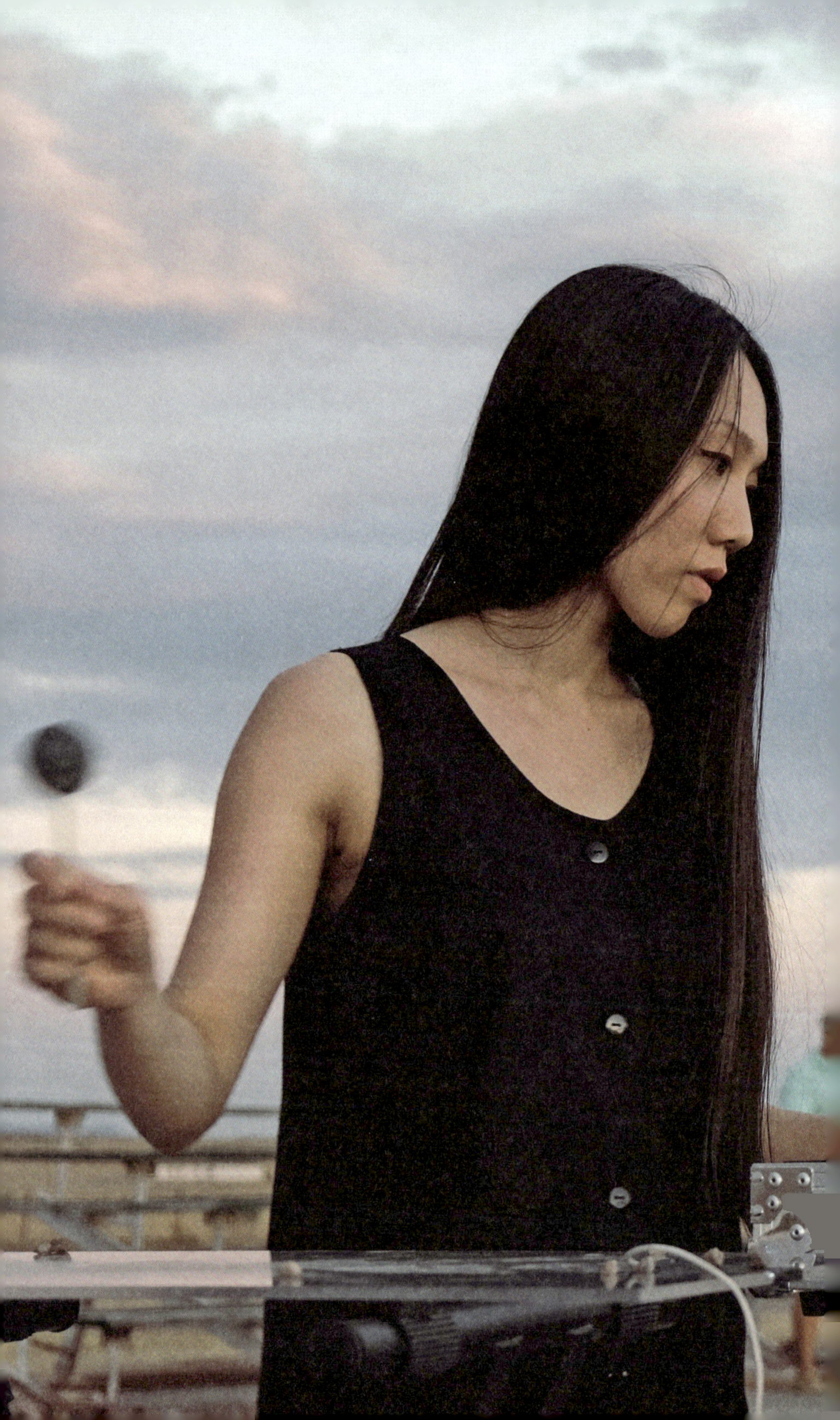

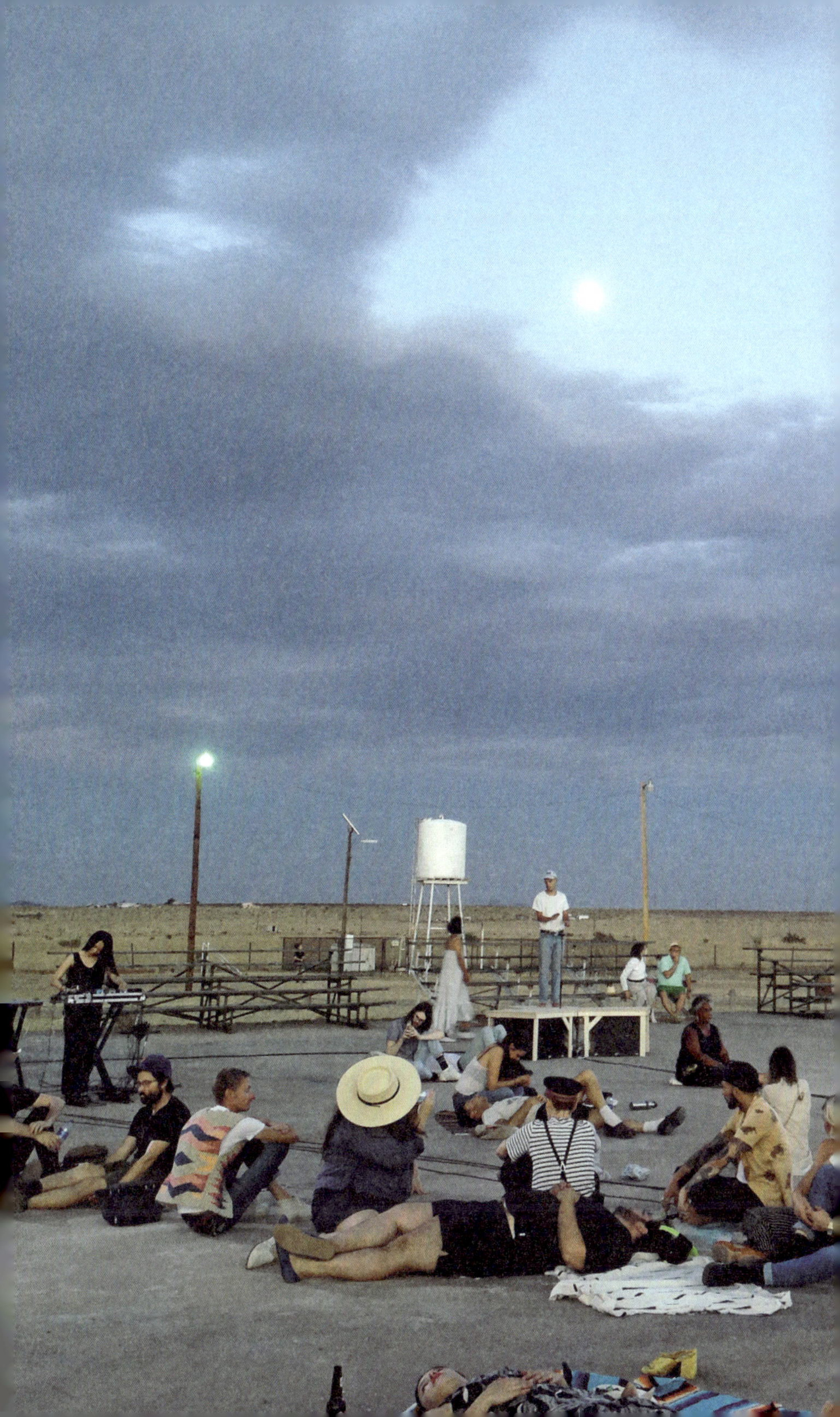

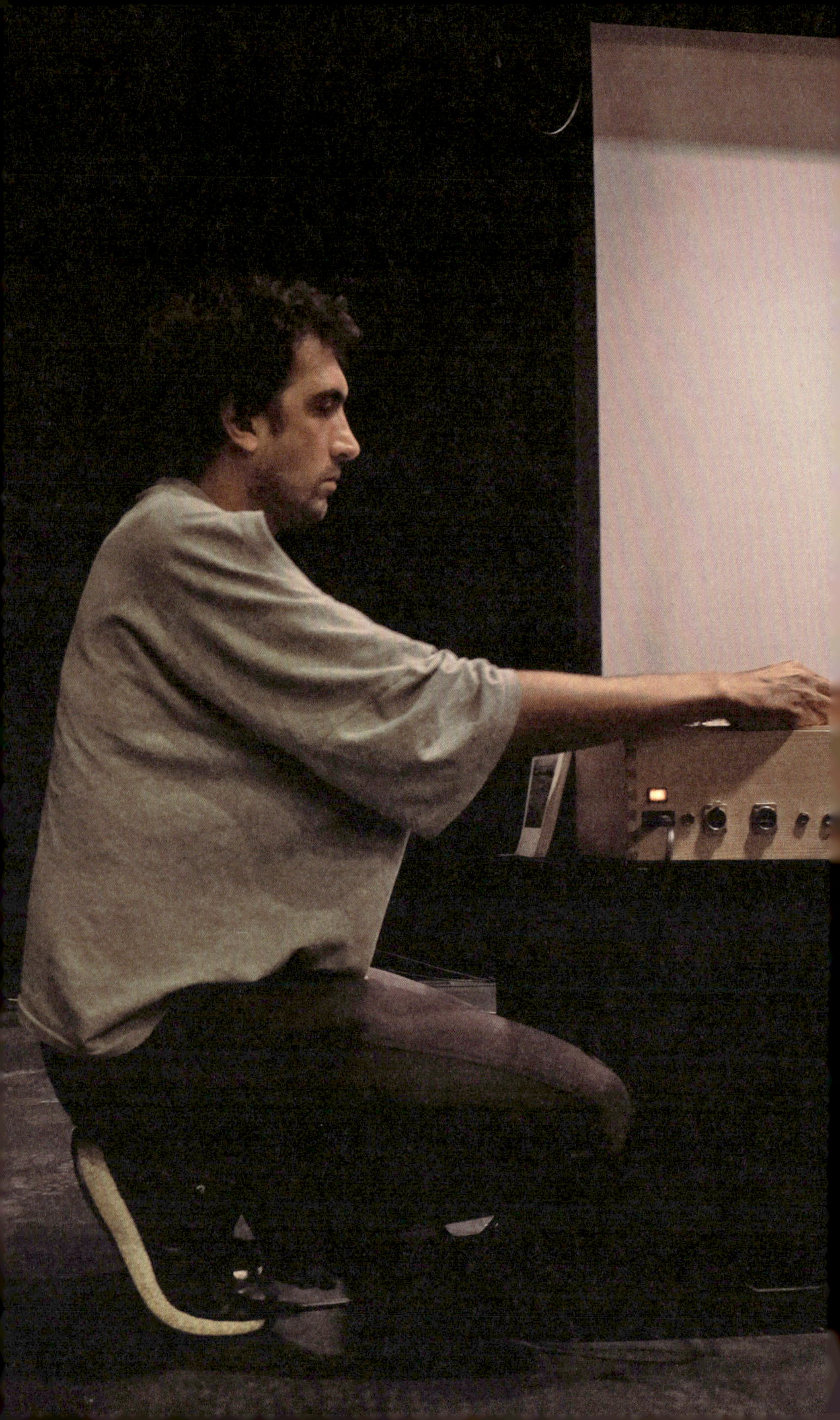

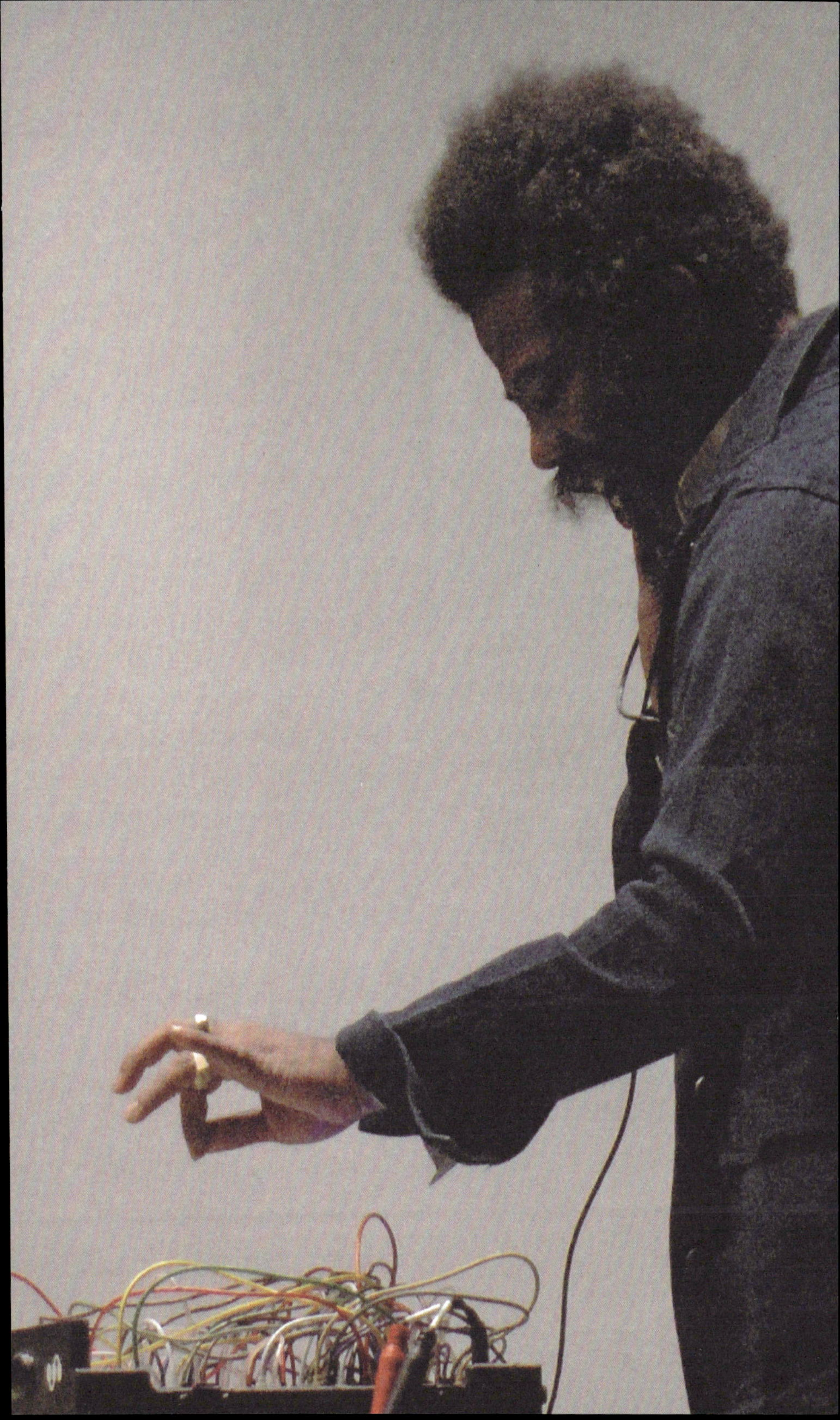

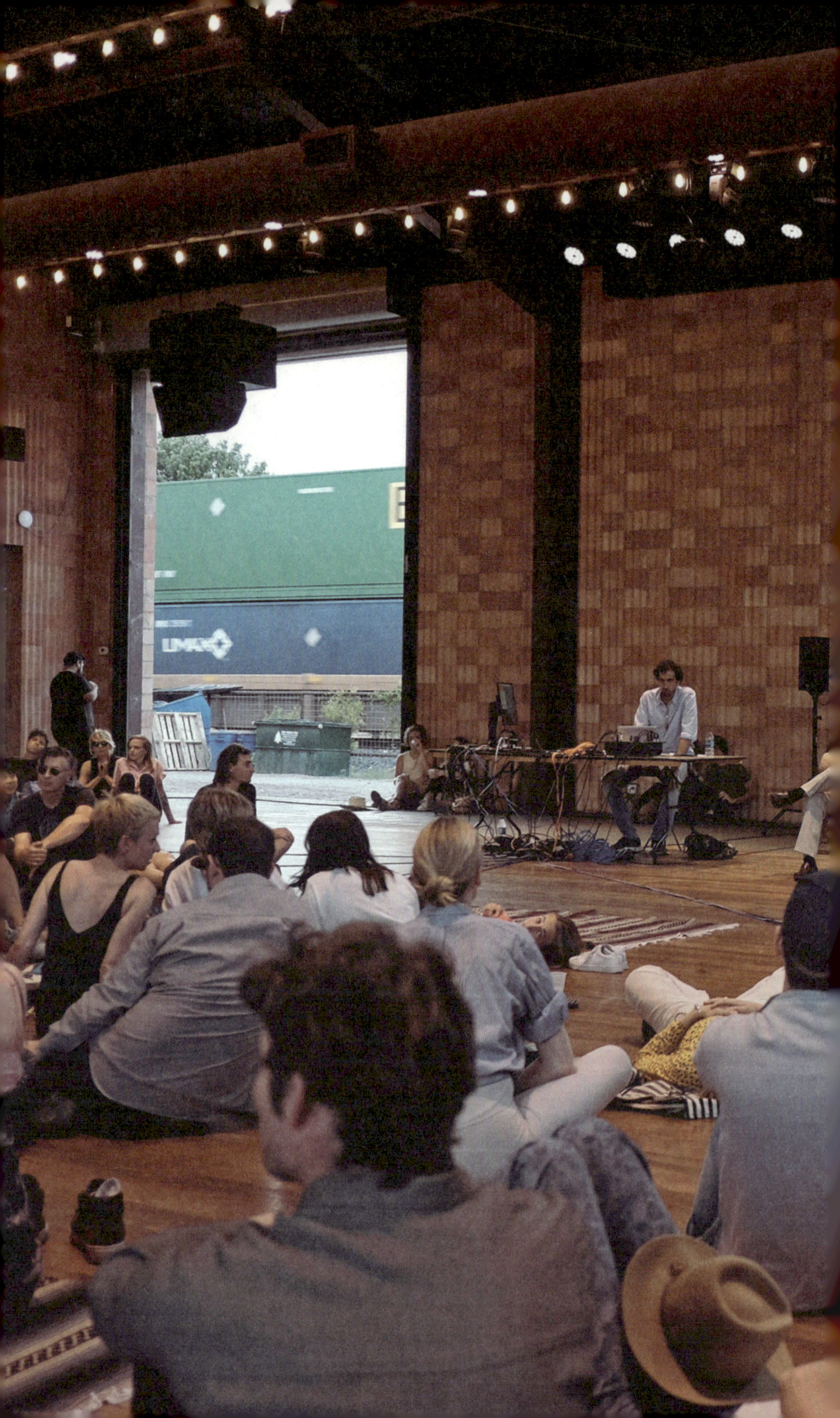

Rain

in

the

Desert

Ian Lewis

The night before Tarek Atoui arrived in Marfa, I dreamt of the sea. I was driving home as the day ended, and features of the landscape were becoming indistinct in the fading light. Beside the road, I saw a cluster of small motorboats and sailboats at harbor. The boats floated in air, suspended above the ground at a waterless-waterline. Anchors, at the ends of taut chains slung over the sides, kept the boats from drifting from their harbor. "Look," I said to a friend suddenly beside me. "You can see how high the water used to be." I often dream of the ocean here; it seems a part of me still struggles to understand how, no matter how long ago, this desert was once a seafloor.

Atoui came to Marfa after travels to actual harbors: Athens, Abu Dhabi, Singapore. There, he made recordings that would be collected in his new instruments, the *Sound Boxes*, one of which he brought to West Texas, hundreds of miles—or millions of years—from the nearest sea. Marfa can feel like a waterfront though, the essential element not the water, but an expanse of nearly untraversable space reaching to the horizon. And to the migrants and refugees that survive the crossing of that great expanse (Marfa lies only sixty miles north of Mexico), like the many thousands that arrive in harbors such as Athens after days at sea, Marfa can be a port, though far from a safe harbor.

As I listened to Atoui's performance in the open expanse of Vizcaino Park, a few miles outside of town, I was thinking about how seas can turn to land and then back again, how populations migrate, and, on a smaller scale, how quickly a small, West Texas town can transform. What can survive such incessant upheaval, incremental and catastrophic? Earlier in the week, Atoui had spoken of his thoughts on the preservation and transmission of art forms—that he does not record or transcribe his performances, stating, paradoxically, that this allows the work to live on. Sometime before reaching the horizon, the sounds of the performance faded into silence.

> I come from Arab culture... an oral culture. It's a culture
> that refused different forms of writing, texts, writing
> music, writing poetry (All quotes from Tarek Atoui come
> from a public talk and performance at the Crowley
> Theater in Marfa on May 25, 2018).

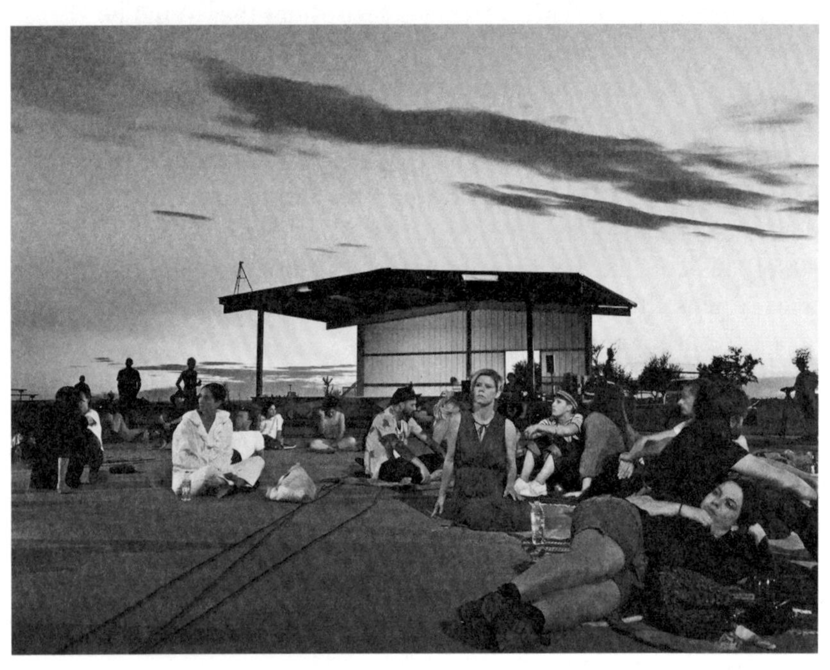

Atoui gives two reasons for working in this tradition—his
refusal to commit works to record: first, so that ideas do not
become individual property but belong to the collective; second, so
that things have the ability to change and adapt to their time and
place, even migrate from one civilization to another. I was struck by
the generosity and trust inherent in these reasons, traits I found
to be embodied by Atoui himself. He invited three other electronic
musicians to share the stage with him during *Marfa Sounding*: his
brother Jad Atoui, as well as Amma Ateria and Robert Aiki Aubrey
Lowe. The other instrument Atoui brought, *0.9*, was originally
created for deaf players and audiences—its frequencies so low they
are felt rather than heard. And here, Atoui invited the audience to
play, letting us explore the resonance of the performance spaces
with this instrument. By focusing only on the immediate experience
for the musicians and audience present, Atoui created something
unique and shared—the best conditions for inspiring others to
further ideas.

> If I want my piece to be preserved and transmitted it is
> trying to find as much as possible the capacity for it to
> generate multiple forms.

Guiding the performance with minimal gestures to the other players,
Atoui highlighted each musician—letting them, in turn, rise above
the rest. There was a moment when Amma Ateria created sounds
like thunder over Atoui's recording of rain in Athens, and I was sure
I smelled actual rainfall, but the sky overhead was free of clouds.

Cloudlike: perhaps that is how I can best describe Tarek
Atoui. Drawing up the world's sounds and ideas only to release
them in a generative rainfall somewhere else. Rain in Singapore
becomes rain in Athens becomes rain in Marfa. A fishmonger in
Athens calls out across the Texas desert. The dry earth soaks
up the rain while the cloud quietly dissipates above, leaving behind
the possibility of growth.

Here in Marfa, it is impossible not to think of the contrast
between Atoui's practice and that of Donald Judd. But if there was
any ambiguity, Atoui made himself clear:

131

As someone coming after Judd... I don't want to create
more forms in this world, fixed forms. I don't want to
create things that are there as monoliths and that just
leave us with the burden of keeping them, sustaining
them like guardians of the temple.

Judd and his institutions in Marfa take up a lot of space: mental
space, textual space, and of course, many buildings. But those that
dedicate themselves to the sustaining of his legacy are not
guardians but contemporaries—still engaged in a dialogue brought
here by Judd. In the last decade, Marfa as art destination became
Marfa as tourist destination and is becoming Marfa as brand
destination. Is it inevitable that The Chinati Foundation becomes a
temple, incomprehensible even to those who guard it—if anyone
cares enough to do that? Perhaps, but sustaining them until then is
no burden. They will be maintained as long as they are generative,
as long as they give back something in exchange for the work put
into them. Judd and his legacy have brought innumerable artists
and ideas to Marfa—his physical, fixed forms marking a gathering
site that makes work like *Marfa Sounding* possible. The town and
world will change around these forms, but the forms will also
change in the eyes of those who view them. In the end, fixed forms
are illusions. Donald Judd had strong beliefs about the permanent
placement of the works at Chinati, but that does not mean he
believed in their permanence. His works reside in a former
artillery shed on a defunct military base, Robert Irwin's on the
grounds of a hospital. Surely the presence of war and sickness, two
realities awaiting anyone harboring dreams of immortality, was not
lost on Judd.

What is important after all is the ability to generate space
for new ideas and work. Through the generosity of Atoui, I was
able to see the generosity of Judd, but most of all, I am better able
to see the generosity of Marfa. Atoui describes his work as a
negotiation between ephemeral and fixed forms, and I cannot
think of a better description of Marfa itself. Here we celebrate
light, the most ephemeral of all, against the fixed geologic
landscape. It was these qualities that attracted Judd, and Marfa's

openness that welcomed him. The same light continuously takes
up tenancy in Judd's works before vacating it again, like ships in
harbors, continuously making the work anew. Perhaps they are
open forms after all, like Marfa. With generosity and trust shown
by those that have long lived here, Marfa has welcomed
opportunity and change, adapting to the times. Atoui's visit was
a reminder that if we hold onto that generosity and trust, we will
welcome the regenerative rainfalls to come.

Gravitating

to Opposites

Amma Ateria

in conversation with

Caitlin Murray

I think of how poet Nathaniel Mackey's describes Ornette Coleman's composition "Embraceable You" in his *Bedouin Hornbook* (1986):

> Tangled up with "Embraceable You" I tend to hear my own heartbeat, amplified and coming at me from outside. It's as though the heart were a ventriloquist of sorts, throwing its voice at an ever more obtuse angle so as to exact an acoustical shell from the surrounding air. It's an eerie feeling to be engulfed by one's own heartbeat, put upon by the heat of one's own stolen pulse like a vulnerable flame palpitating in a draft. The heart's thrown voice, it seems, moves as a mutable window or a "mute" succession of windows, the transparent advance of an elliptical witness to a many-tongued yet unmentionable, all the more audacious truth. It appears to elope with each evaporative cranial kiss or breathy phantom caress as with an outrageous, caged or cagey embrace—caught up in the ache or the echoed report of its eventual extinction. It's as if the stolen pulse fed the amputated hand with which one might one day stroke the ribs of a ghost.

I think that Amma Ateria's sounds reside in this tangle—in a sonic utopic non-place in extremis. Her sounds embrace the pounding inextricability of interiority and exteriority. They vacillate, conjoin, and overpower as they retreat into silence. Perhaps this is what Amma Ateria means when she says:

> I focus in the many inversions I can create to transition from one end to another, in pursuit of a coexistence of polarity.

The physicality of gravity, the grace of the void, their entanglement, and the sounds they make. My conversation with Amma Ateria began in person in Marfa in May 2018 at the time of her *Marfa Sounding* performances. We continued the conversation by email over the summer and into the fall, where it began to take concrete form.

135

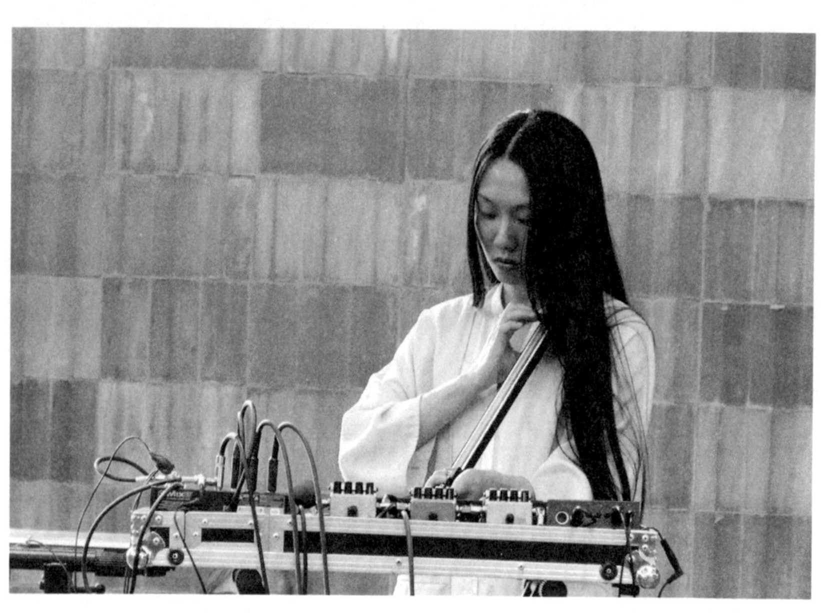

CAITLIN MURRAY   I thought that maybe we could begin with a question about the palette of sounds that you work with. As we know, painters work with very specific color palettes: Classical Greek painting used red, white, and black; Vermeer is known for using yellows; Poussin for blue; and Rembrandt brown. Is there a way to describe the kinds of sounds that make up your palette and the kinds of sounds that you are particularly interested in right now?

AMMA ATERIA   I always want to create a sense of duality, so I gravitate to sounds that allow me to express opposing ends: sounds that depict the urgency of flight paired with sounds floating lightly in the air; they remind me of a time when I had my first experiences of polar opposites. My palette consists of various timbre of white, pink, red, and brown noise; they are the foundation for me to synthetically replicate natural sounds of air pressure with modulation of depth, motion, and behavior assignments... such as the back and forth repetitions of water waves that are both calm and violent, or a close-range airplane flying at impossible distance and speed. I study and create various industrial concrete sounds that allow me to compose sonic phrases in performance: sounds of different materials like the swelling friction of metallic surfaces, deep sustained sounds of glass that transform to the verge of piercing, the gravity of falling objects, the many variations of water, soft throbbing engines, inaudible conversations, the speed in air. I am also interested in the human heartbeat right now; there are so many variations of the same rhythm. I use silence a lot too; I think space is as important as what is visible, and I need it for balance.

I want to understand how sound is perceived with physicality in the human experience. I'm interested in expanding the human experience by extending the parameters of sound in its color, velocity, and loudness: an outcome that is minimal in context, but which triggers an overwhelming response. I think to myself, how does pressure travel through air, what shapes of waveform does it take, where does the frequency range fall, and how can I magnify it? How could it

evolve, how does it move? Through expanding the boundaries
of the sonic spectrum's intensity and softness at once, I am
able to create transitions and variations to rearrange the
reality I know, reflecting ever-changing states of entropy. I
feel that there is something rebellious in my act of creating
chaos by taking up opposing positions, and some sort of
harmony as I allow the two opposing points to coexist and
engage in equal loudness and visibility.

Something that fascinates me and became part of my
sound palette is the subjective perception of equal loudness.
In coexistence, when low frequencies are very loud, let's
say a throbbing low rumble in 20–50Hz at 90dB, higher
frequencies such as 10k–20kHz at 15dB need only
a fraction of the amplitude in relation to have visibility when
introduced. The two opposing points of sound are quite
simple on their own, appearing within themselves in their
own space, their frequency range. It is the engagement
between the two points that becomes complex, creating a
gray area, and how I want to see them resolve back into a
cadence of silence.

CM   Could you describe your first cognizant experience of polarity?
Was this a sonic experience?

AA   It came to me in images through a silent dream I had when
I was five, and then again in reality on rooftops in Hong
Kong with overwhelming sights and sounds of close-range
airplanes. I think those are my earliest memories. The
dream consists of a violent charcoal magnetic substance,
these small particles that behaved so violently with urgency,
from the lower-left corner within my peripheral, moving
coarsely and diagonally across my vision until it takes over
a whole rectangular shape. I remember that it was
frightening, but after a while of complete darkness, I felt
calm. What follows is a pale white milky substance that
washes over slowly and effortlessly from the facing
direction until it took over the whole rectangular shape. I
can't recall which color begins the process, but these

occurrences of opposing movements, intentions, colors, repeat themselves endlessly. It was like a cinema in my mind with a minimal plot. So when I was in Marfa, as I walked into Robert Irwin's work *untitled (dawn to dusk)*, which was inaugurated in 2016 after 17 years of planning, I felt as if I was walking into the three dimensionality of that dream. I wanted to experience walking through it back and forth, again and again. Something about this back-and-forth-ness brings me comfort and understanding of how to exist and navigate oppositions.

The visceral experience of polar opposites happened to me during those same early years in Hong Kong. My father used to bring me to different residential rooftops to count the stars; it was the first time I understood the concept of infinity and repetition. One of the rooftops was near the old Hong Kong Kai Tak Airport. This was in the late 1980s, so the airport was still adjacent to residential areas until it closed in 1998 and moved thirty kilometers west. At landing, the aircrafts flew incredibly close above us; I thought I could touch them as it took over my vision. It was the first time I experienced two extremes of physicality and emotions through sound and vision. The comforting fascination of the night sky, and the intense noise from close proximity, was deafening and thrilling. I can still remember these feelings, the embodiment of loudness: it expanded my threshold of fear and fascination. These feelings have stuck with me forever and shaped my way of seeing. It was shocking to me at the time as a child, even as an adult when I visited Hong Kong in 1997 for the transfer of sovereignty from the United Kingdom to China, which was the last time I experienced those airplanes in person, one year prior to the closing of the airport. It was really meaningful to me when Tarek Atoui presented sounds he collected from different parts of the world during his project with *Marfa Sounding*, the way he brought spaces together. I appreciated that experience of performing with him, as I emulate the sound of flights in Hong Kong.

CM   In reference to your desire to expand "the human experience
      by extending the parameters of sounds," in what way do you
      think that human experience should be expanded? Towards
      what and/or away from what do you want to move people?
      Why is that important to your work?

AA   I often find myself in encounter with moments of polarity
      that bring me consciousness in extreme directions. These
      tokens of polarity are to me stimuli that activate new
      psychophysical perceptions. I need these moving moments,
      experiences that expand my threshold of senses. This is the
      notion I carry with me in my performances.

      Knowing how each sound begins and develops in time
      is important to me. There is something grounding in always
      knowing the unambiguous form of a sound in its simple clear
      expression, so my mind can apply or recognize the changes.
      I think there is something worthwhile about this way of
      knowing. As I work through permutations, it allows the
      listener to engage in modulation through their own changing
      states and perception. When one's heartbeat accelerates
      through a sonic experience, it mimics a state of panic,
      a sort of fictional fear. Such an experience creates a state
      of expansion, expanding the threshold of consciousness,
      boundaries, widening of spectrums, and away from the
      notion of limitations when there is little to work with.

      I want to give experiences of what it is like to coexist
      with oppositions in frequencies, and what that means in the
      context of being human. How do you coexist with someone
      or something in opposition from you? Does it make you
      appear stronger, more defined, or does it diminish you?
      I think as a human being, it is important to know how to
      coexist and navigate with polarities; I myself learn how to
      do so through sound.

CM   Your performance in Marfa was very physical in the sense of
      how you play. Additionally, there are the ways in which the
      human body performs, such as the cardiac cycle—the
      heartbeat—the relationship between the physicality of your

140

performance and its effect on the "performance" of the listener's body.

AA   In Marfa, I was interested in the wooden material, the architecture and vibration of the theater. I wanted to create movement with stillness. When I am standing still, I become aware of how my heartbeat moves me. The subtlety of heartbeat is monumental to me; it is always present, always coexisting with something. Thus, my attempt to emulate the heartbeat extends with accelerating intensity and vibrates with the space we are in, where the architectural space and the listener's body becomes a part of the sound.

When I began to learn about improvisation, my experiences were only with acoustic musicians. The challenge of entering and exiting with electronic sounds while playing with acoustic musicians was really fascinating to me. There are dynamics that a violinist, cellist, or percussionist would make that are so immediate and raw. The way they utilize their bodies for sonic response was something I resonated with. This urgency of physical output through gestures is something I adapted to and require. It feels quite exposed but liberating at once, like out of hiding, and out of the dark.

CM   Can you talk about your use of the ribbon controller as an instrument? What does the ribbon controller allow for you in terms of physicality?

AA   I gravitate to electronic instruments with tactile control and behavior assignment abilities, so that it can become an extension of my body. With the ribbon controller, I simultaneously control voltage with modular synths and trigger sound palettes through MIDI with bodily gestures. Each sound has its own unique assignment of parameters in frequency range, number of voices, repetitions, output channel, envelope, and reverberation time. Each sound palette represents a different space. The ribbon controller becomes an extension of my body when I carry it in my arms and near my torso. As I trigger ribbon's surface, I am able to develop muscle memory. I assign sounds to positions on the

ribbon controller by correlating them to my own sense of
positions as I recall the tension and release I want to express
in the contemporary moment. It allows me to have a cross-
modal synesthetic experience.

CM   Can you discuss the major influences on your work?

AA   The first moment I felt connected to someone in the way I
saw and categorized sound was Italian futurist Luigi Russolo,
I had a secret life for seven years where I was creating sounds
I never shared with anyone, until I came across his 1913
manifesto *L'arte dei rumori* (The Art of Noises). Learning
about Russolo's *intonarumori* (experimental noise machines)
and reading his manifesto gave me a sense of belonging; I
carried it with me for a couple years like a bible while I was
searching for my own perspectives, which was when I began
to recall the sounds of aircrafts from my childhood. Another
big influence is the 1882 novella by Edwin A. Abbott *Flatland:
A Romance of Many Dimensions,* which continues to inspire
me. I really understood the violent outbursts from the sharp
forms of women in *Flatland,* so I felt a need to interpret them.
The explosive and silence sonic phrases I choose are relevant
to the pressure accumulated from invisibility in the second
dimension, where the women's bodies are lines that do not
take any shape. I was also fascinated by how the inhabitants
utilized sound for localization; it made me think a lot about
space and distance, the compression and expansion of sound
in a two-dimensional space versus a three-dimensional space.
And although it was not a literature about feminism, it
introduced me to the perception of the so-called second sex,
and led me to reflect on and draw connections with my own
paradigm through sound.

My greatest mentor is composer and flutist Maggi
Payne; it was with her that I began focusing on sound
synthesis. Iannis Xenakis, a Greek-French composer and
architect, and Galina Ukoskaya, a Russian composer and
pianist: they both lived through WWII and created piercing
work after times of devastation and destruction. Both of their

works are so corporeal to me, I feel so much from listening to them. Arvo Pärt introduced me to a state of surrender I am not familiar with, but very much want. And filmmaker Paul Clipson; through his work I began to exist with sound and in the world in a beautiful way that I didn't know could exist. He taught me stillness that is at the same time rapidly moving, how something very small could be held closely, how something monumental could be felt even when far away.

No Room For Quiet:

Environmental Responses

Jad Atoui
in conversation with

Claire Amiot

I participated in *Marfa Sounding* as an art student in residence at Fieldwork Marfa. I had the opportunity to play the *0.9*—an instrument created by Tarek Atoui—during two live performances. I met Jad Atoui during a public workshop where he was presenting his work on an analog machine. But my first real encounter with Jad's music was during the first evening of performances at the Crowley Theatre. It was a few minutes after I had arrived and before the series of individual performances started. People were chatting as they were waiting in the hall, and I started to hear some sounds: long, low, and undulating frequencies merging with the constant hubbub of people's voices. From time to time a high pitch, like an electrical signal would be heard. In the darkness of the room, the electronic music coming from Jad's modular synthesizers and the natural sound of the theatre seemed to be in conversation and revealing each other. A discreet presence: that is what I feel when I listen to Jad's music and when I see him play. Whether through his performances or his work in composition, Jad uses music as a tool to reveal impalpable and invisible energies of his outer and inner environment.

CLAIRE AMIOT   At the occasion of *Marfa Sounding,* which took place from May 25 to May 27 2018, you collaborated on a series of performances conceived and organized by your brother Tarek Atoui alongside two others musicians: Robert Aiki Aubrey Lowe and Amma Ateria. Can you tell us about your understanding of this overall project and your role within it?

JAD ATOUI   WITHIN is a project that combines different sound-related practices into one body of work. Tarek created two instruments, *Sound Boxes* and the *0.9,* which are both software-based instruments. The *Sound Boxes* are based on recordings taken from harbors around the world and the idea is to use and manipulate these concrete sounds in an improvisational context. The *0.9* is taken from a different project that Tarek worked on. It is an instrument that allows people with hearing disabilities to perform and take part in an improvised concert. These two instruments were created using different approaches, but they have strong similarities when it comes to their performance values. My approach is different, as I do not work with digital but rather with analog instruments. I work with a modular synthesizer where electricity is the basis of the sound, incorporating other sounds or projects based on analog systems. But to answer your question: my role in this project was to perform with my own instruments while letting Tarek's input and the spaces we were in somehow "control" or take over the performance.

CA   In the week preceding the events, Tarek Atoui organized a series of workshops in which you were involved. Two workshops were open to the general public, and two addressed high school students from the Marfa Independent School District. Can you tell us more about these workshops? How do you work with people discovering electroacoustic materials for the first time? And do these questions of transmission and pedagogy operate in your own work?

JA   During these workshops, Tarek explained the digital processes of music making and music production as well as the incorporation of sensors and software into a composition process. I presented the analog side of music composition, explaining the basics of analog synthesizers and how to use them in order to create sound and compose music. My instrument contains different modules. Each module has a specific role when it comes to sound. Let's say it is like a box that contains around twenty mini-instruments. For example, I have one module that generates sound, another one that produces effects, and I combine these elements together when I play.

CA   I was wondering about your influences. How do you relate to traditions in experimental music, serialism, and Minimalism explored in previous years of *Marfa Sounding*? You grew up in Lebanon in a context of war before moving to New York to study sound engineering and design. The historical, political, and social contexts of Lebanon and New York are radically different, as is the history of music in these two places. Can

146

Staff 1: Piano
Staff 2: Viola
Staff 3: Cello
Staff 4: Bass & Drums

X: Time
Y: Pitch

Piano:

——————— : pitch range
●——————— : louder / struck

Viola:

——————— : pitch range
« : play range in between
… : pizzicato

Cello:

——————— : pitch range
« : play range in between
… : pizzicato

Bass:

:::: : short decay
● : loud
○ : soft
⊗ : rhythmic / melodic
— : drone

Drums:

Refer to solo piece instructions sheet

Alocasia Poly reponse to Ph4

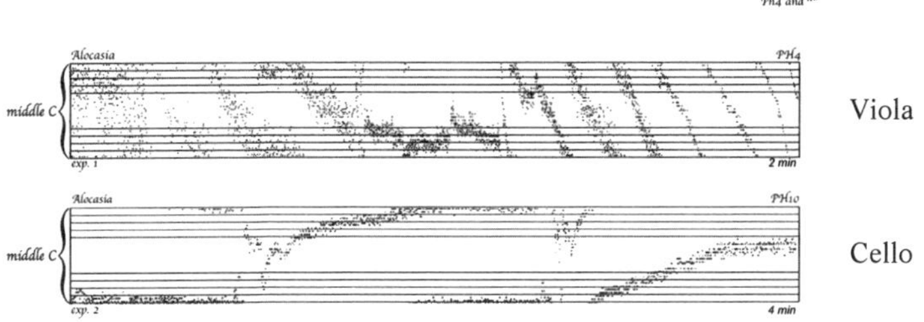

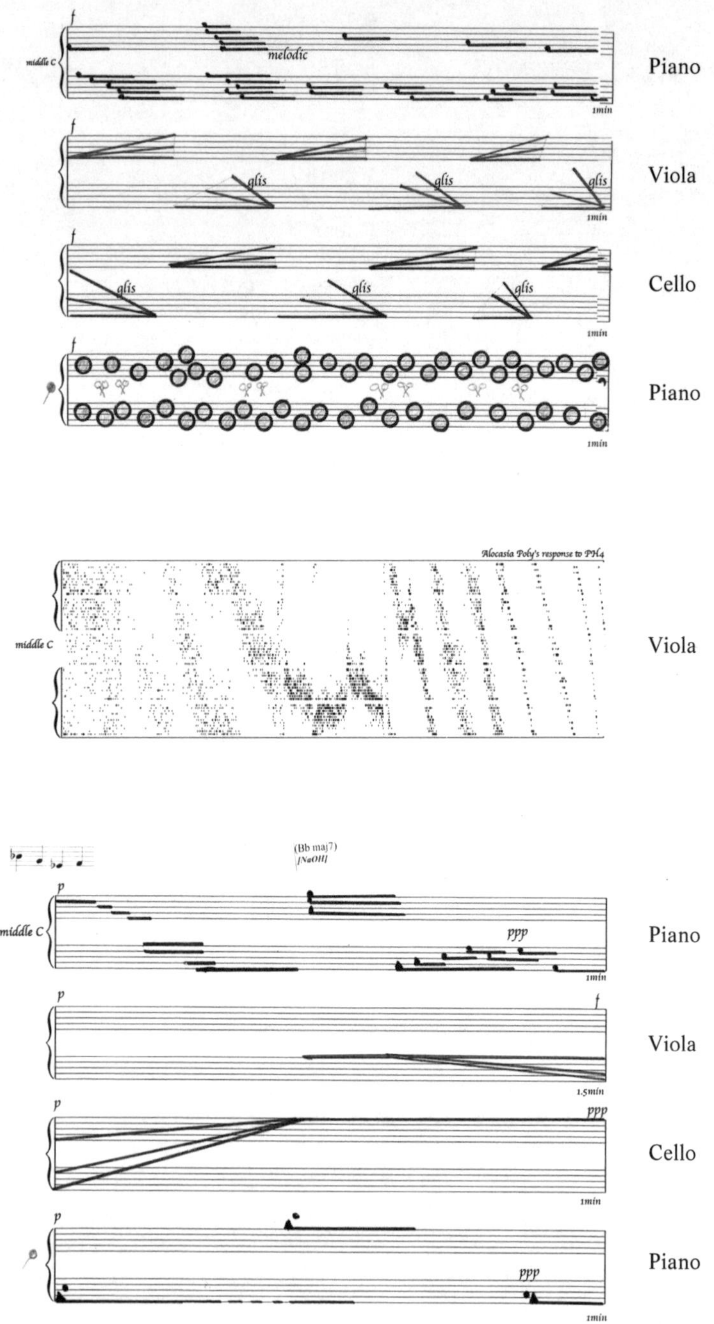

Jad Atoui, *Alocasia Poly reponse to Ph4*. Courtesy of the artist

you tell us more about the impact this geographic movement has had on both your creation process and your music?

JA I have been very much influenced by Minimalist musicians such as Steve Reich, Terry Riley, or Philip Glass, all of whom taught me that within repetition you have changes through time. My compositions are more and more minimalist in this way. I use very simple elements that repeat and change gradually over time. The spaces I work with also have a strong influence. In Marfa, the natural elements naturally integrated into our improvisation. We did not have to force them. These sounds invited us to play with them.

When I arrived in New York from Beirut, I was exposed to new types of sound and to a noise-filled environment. In New York there is no room for quiet. Not only the sounds of the intense metropolis—cars, construction, different accents, and languages—but also things like trains. In Beirut there are no trains. In New York I would take the train every day, and it changed the way I played or the way I perceive music and sounds in general. Every city has its own sonic identity, and New York is a very rich sonic world. A composition not only reflects our deepest emotions or a combination of narrative and mathematical theories, but also an unconsciousness that is similar to a sponge. The aspects of our environment that we absorb inadvertently become embedded in us and affect our behavior, performance, and output. As a musician, I feel that each time I play, I respond to both my immediate and extended environments; that part of an "inner" me that captures hidden signals drives the performance.

In New York I also started to improvise by working with many jazz musicians from the New York scene, who were themselves inspired by the city and the intensity of its sonic presence. They taught me how to react and integrate this environment into the music I produce. One of my major sources of inspiration is John Zorn, whom I consider my musical mentor. I started volunteering at The Stone, and we started improvising together. He taught me a lot about music; through him I was able to play with many other musicians,

like Laurie Anderson for example. Jazz and experimental
music, and the combination of the two at The Stone, has been
a great influence. I also admire the work of Herbie Hancock,
who was one of the first to associate analog music with jazz.

CA   Before each performance in Marfa, Tarek shared a score with
you and the other musicians that established the timing of
each intervention, the collective moments, and the solo parts.
This score acted as a skeleton upon which to improvise. How
do you work with improvisation? Do you always have a
system in mind or is it sometimes more intuitive?

JA   For me, improvisation can be done through either an intuitive
or a planned approach. And sometimes they cross each other.
Some of my improvisational work is based on graphic scores
where the performers are given certain rules and conditions
in which to work and improvise (the same method that Tarek
uses). But most importantly, improvisation demands an acute
understanding of the relation between yourself and what
is happening around you: between stimuli and output. It is
a performance of not only giving but also receiving the
environment by analyzing and understanding its rhythmic
energies—that is, by putting yourself in a state of
unpredictability where the listening skills and receptivity to
changes drive the performance and the relationship between
the performer and its environment leads the behavior,
performance, and creation process.

I like to play in unusual spaces or settings where music
becomes part of what is happening. I like to play sound in the
background; it also takes away the pressure of performance
and allows for more experimentation. I often play in
exhibitions or similar kinds of contexts, which is the benefit
of working with an analog instrument: as long as you can find
electricity you can take it basically anywhere.

CA   Last November, you performed at L'Eglise Saint-Merri in Paris:
a space that has a lot of resonance and hence quickly saturates
in sound. The two performance sites in Marfa—Saint George

Hall and Vizcaino Park—seem to be the opposite: the desert has almost no resonance. An unbounded space: the scale and flatness of the location opened to a plurality of recognizable sounds. At Saint George Hall, the sound of the train passing directly behind the location during the performance was especially strong. What role does landscape play when you perform or compose music, and what impact did the specificity of Marfa's outdoor locations have on your performance?

JA When I played at L'Eglise Saint-Merri, there was a lot of resonance that deeply affected the performance: the machine had to adapt to the space. In a way, Marfa was a similar case. The space was leading the performance. When we were working at Saint George Hall and the train passed a few meters from us, it became part of the composition; the event leads to a certain type of reaction and that reaction can then be translated into sound.

I believe, without exaggeration, that the performance at Vizcaino Park was one of my favorite moments as a performer. I felt really comfortable with the environment that surrounded us. At some point in the performance I stopped playing and walked around to capture what was happening with the other performers. The relation between the landscape and all of us, as musicians, was very special. I felt we were fully part of the setting and that the composition unfolded in a very smooth way and was charged with a lot of feeling. All this was also due to the way Tarek developed the composition. The field recordings of the *Sounds Boxes* were used to control our sounds, so the natural and concrete sounds of both the boxes and the environment were controlling our dynamics and frequencies, rather than the other way around. This was very special because usually you feel that you control the sound you produce, but during this performance it was the opposite: we were controlled by the sound.

CA *Sound Boxes* create a unique sonic palette via sound samples recorded in different harbors around the world, such as Athens, Abu Dhabi, and Singapore. In some of your works,

151

like the *Black Sea Series* album (2014), which incorporates field recordings collected since 2011, we can recognize the steps of someone walking, birdsong, and human voices. What is the relationship between these figurative sounds and "abstract" electronic sounds in your work?

JA   When I started playing music in 2010 and 2011, my first instruments were field recordings. I used to record sounds from the sea or from different parts of the city and then integrate them within the synthesizer. This is exactly what Tarek did in Marfa with the *Sound Boxes*: a combination of natural sounds and modular synthesizer.

Black Sea Series is a sequence of tracks made of sounds extracted from the sea (wave sounds, stone sounds, etc.). It turned out to be a dark and sad music. In any composition, there are three kinds of frequencies: low frequencies, limit frequencies, and high frequencies. I knew you could find all three frequencies in field recordings, so I started to cut and distribute these recordings according to those categories (deep sounds from the water being the base, beats taken out of stone sounds, and melodies from the wave sounds). In this earlier work, some of the original sound sources are recognizable; but now, even when I am working with concrete sounds, I transform them so they are completely abstract and unrecognizable.

Usually my work starts with an idea driven by different sources of inspiration: it can be an image, a workshop I did, a film, or even a scientific process. When I compose at home, it always starts with an image. For example, the track "Diving Blue" [released on the 2019 album *Anthology of Electroacoustic Lebanese Music*] came from a personal experience: being in the sea in Lebanon with a strong water current that made me lose control and be swept away by waves. But sometimes it starts with an idea that unfolds in time, leading to an in-depth exploration in sounds, technics, and media.

CA   You create scores that are almost drawings. How do you value these documents? Is the purpose of a score to be played or interpreted? As a composer, do you let the scores be interpreted by other musicians?

JA   Graphic scores are one of the most appealing media for composition. You can translate anything into graphic scores: you can track the movement of a car, take the shape of buildings, write down values such as speed and direction and then assign these values to different shapes and drawings; you can use drawings, colors, shapes... It is basically unlimited. It is also an interesting way to combine visuals with sounds or to depart from a visual in order to generate sound. What I really like about graphic scores is their capacity to act as an international language. They allow you to communicate ideas and translate precisely what is in your mind to an image that any musician can read. Musicians will then interpret these drawings, as most scores are interpreted and not played. This process creates music that sounds different every time it is performed, like a living entity that evolves and changes with each new performance and performer.

CA   In 2015, you started to work on your *Biosonics* project: a three-year collaboration with molecular biologist Ivan Marazzi. Can you explain this project and how it started?

JA   The aim of *Biosonics* was to use biological data to generate sonic compositions. It began with the following idea: like humans, the behavior of lower life forms is also influenced by their surroundings, and their resulting conditions expressed through biological reactions. As a futuristic iteration of this concept, we decided to experiment in giving voice to biological data extracted from life forms, i.e. plants, and model their biological response to the environment into music, thus generating compositions that are written by plants and played by humans.

In the first iteration of this concept, we used the perturbation of a simple biological system to generate music. We leveraged the fact that plants respond to environmental changes by generating micro-variations in electrical conductivity that can be measured by testers such as the Midi

Sprout. Using this system, we recorded the behavior of
plants under different chemical stimulations that mimic
environmental changes (e.g., sun exposure, rain, darkness).
The plant responses were then transformed into graphic
scores for musicians to play. And this translation of
scientific and biological data into sound actually led to better
understanding of some scientific facts through auditory
experiences. For example, we know that if we hear a high-
pitched sound it means that a plant has more acidity.
Listening is a language: it communicates information, ideas,
and scientific facts.

CA   In *Biosonics,* science and performance are intrinsically
linked. Could you explain a bit more about how this works
technically? And then, more conceptually, what does it
mean to you to play music with biological forms and sounds
that are usually outside of human reach?

JA   In terms of technical process, we came up with the idea to
prescribe a series of injections with substances that mimic
normal changes in the biological and environmental status of
some plants in order to induce a cellular response that can
be monitored as conductivity change. Different plants, such
as aloe vera and prickly pear (cactus strain), were used based
on their known fast responsiveness to biological fluxes
because they are water-based. In principle, the experiments
were designed to influence the plant's electrical activity in
a controlled environment. We first conducted preliminary
experiments by using single injections of one chemical at
a time, which allowed us to monitor the biological changes
in the plant, lag times of the response, and the refractory
behavior to subsequent injections. This then served as
a baseline to catalog responsiveness based on the identity of
the substances. For example, substances that mimic rain
(increase in water absorption) induced a dynamic response
that translated into a music crescendo. Substances that mimic
a sunny and dry day would generate low pitch sounds with
intermittent pauses. We then used stimulation altered by

154

different chemicals to model rapid changes and provide a biological multisensory experience that could be translated into dynamic music.

The information gathered, such as Midi notes and the intensity of the electrical pulse, was later used to generate "compositive" profiles. In addition to collaborating with a scientist specialized in perturbations, I worked with an engineer to build sensors that could translate the voltage of the plants into a language that my synthesizer could understand. I also worked with a composer to translate certain sounds into basic scores for musicians (violinists, pianists, bassists, drummers), adapting the instruments to the idea. Through this project, sound was used as a medium to study biological events: composition and performance an illustration of the behavioral science of living beings.

Biosonics uses the natural electricity produced by plants without having to rely on any software. This is what is exciting about analog machines like a modular synthesizer: you can create your own compilation of instruments by combining every module (some that I buy and some that I construct from scratch) in a way that will generate the exact sound you are looking for. Hence each analog musician has her or his own sonic identity. My synthesizer is just a medium, not the source.

Ways to move inside

over,   and

over,

                and

over

Robert Aiki Aubrey Lowe
in conversation with

Anthony Elms

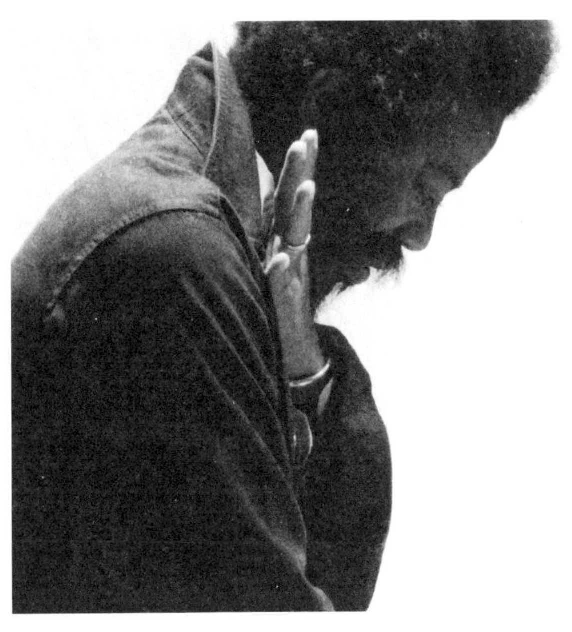

My first awareness of Rob was as a soundman at the Empty Bottle music venue in Chicago. He was behind the soundboard for some of my fondest and most joyous musical experiences. It wasn't too much later that he was responsible for many more joyous moments himself as performer. Often solo under the name Lichens, sometimes in tandem with groups such as White/Light, or various one-offs, like the reverberating night in February 2007 as a member of Rhys Chatham & His Guitar Trio All-Stars. Later, I had the pleasure to in some small way return the favor for all the sounds, co-hosting him in 2016 for a concert where he performed through Philadelphia's House of Roots sound system. With the visual artist Rose Kallal, with whom he has previously collaborated on two books and one recording, he runs Aventures, ltd., a press that explores expanded forms of sound and visual works. They have produced limited editions with Suzanne Ciani, Sarah Davachi, Angel Oloshove, Nathaniel Russell, Hillery Sklar, and Megan Snowe, among others. Harkening back to his training as a visual artist, Lowe has in recent years incorporated his own generatively constructed videos in his live performances. This interview was conducted over two hours in April 2019 at Baby Skips in Bushwick. Below is an edited version.

ANTHONY ELMS   You consciously lay low. Having experienced a lot
    of improvised musical performance, [I'd say] there are a lot
    of people who try to "rise" to the occasion. By which I mean:
    more singularly assert their voice. But you're thinking less
    of singularity. The group is a form to step back and think
    about how you can be embedded in pattern.
ROBERT AIKI AUBREY LOWE   Exactly. And this is something that I
    feel that most people don't understand about improvisation:
    Improvisation is about listening. It doesn't necessarily need to
    be propulsive and battering, which I think a lot of people
    misunderstand about the concept of free improvised music.
    Because a lot of it is a bunch of clatter, and it's ultimately
    uninteresting because they're not listening. You can flex
    whatever muscle you have and be as loud as you can in your
    "solo," or in this idea of call and response, but I don't think

it's actually that. I think people don't understand how to
listen and how to navigate space with others. I feel that it's
really unfortunate, because there's always so much room
to find interesting languages and develop ideas, but people
are not doing that because they're not listening. And so,
when I work in collaboration, I will pull back more and find
the appropriate space.

AE   I've never felt your live performances—when you're in
collaboration—share quite the same quality as your solo records.
The records have a really slow buildup and/or a loud attentive
field of patterning. Something distinct happens and extends.
But when I see you perform collaboratively, sometimes it is not
clear where you are. Like this last Sunday (March 24, 2019, a
concert presented by Ars Nova Workshop at Johnny Brenda's)
in the Yunohana Variations trio with YoshimiO and Susie
Ibarra, there were certain times when you were curtaining
behind the two of them, I would almost say.

RAAL It can be difficult in a space when two drum kits are going
through a PA and the synthesizer's also going through the PA.
When either of them really digs into the drum, it's hard to
understand what's happening. But also, as a trio we've come
into this way of being where the sonic elements that I'm
producing throughout the performance, the things that I'm
investigating, are very percussive; due to the nature of how
I make the sounds, they give the illusion of acoustic
instruments. That's a really nice illusion to put in front of an
audience, because at certain times they can't tell who's doing
what. Certain elements I am providing the audience with
one would assume are the drums, but it's actually the
synthesizer. It's nice to be able to play with that and really
have the trio be something that is sonically very unified,
because what you're processing... you don't necessarily
understand where it's coming from.

AE   So you consider yourself an improviser?
RAAL Absolutely.

159

AE   Even in the solo work, you're an improviser?

RAAL Absolutely. Yeah. I absolutely identify as an improviser who works primarily with voice and a modular synthesizer. There are two ways I view the modular synthesizer: one is as a collaborator; and one is as an extension of my own body, because a lot of my work is very gestural.... The synthesizer lends itself to gesture. There will be elements or behaviors that may be recognizable from other engagements, but it will never be the same. I make sure of that by setting up the synthesizer in different ways every time. It's never exactly the same set-up.

AE   Let's consider that space of gesture and difference. My head is right now in Tony Conrad land. Currently at the ICA [Institute of Contemporary Art, University of Pennsylvania], we have the show *Introducing Tony Conrad: A Retrospective*. With this in mind, there's improvisation as we often think of it, which comes from jazz, with call-and-response, soloing, interlocking, and exuberance. You might call this instant composing—building structure on-site and in-time through progression—for lack of a better, readymade definition. But there's another way of seeing improvising, with the space not for progression but for a static circling and architectural structure. Conrad often talks about it as almost mining into sound. You're actually digging in, excavating, and investigating how the sound is functioning as you make it. Do you identify more as working within—burrowing into the sound—or are you going somewhere: an in-time progressive response? Does this dichotomy interest you?

RAAL No. What I consider most within the realm of performance is creating a space within a space, the idea of transformation. For me, it's most interesting to investigate the actual, physical space upon entering it, and then to transform that space— almost thinking about things architecturally, physically: how to create another landscape or another world inside a space that already exists. Within that space, the witness to performance is transported to another place inside of that space....

160

AE   You're talking about the architecture for the sound?

RAAL   Absolutely. And that also comes with the ritual of dressing the staging, using the African wax that I do in my set-up to create another landscape.

AE   I wanted to ask about the cloth. Glad you brought it up.

RAAL   When I was artist in residence at EMPAC [Curtis R. Priem Experimental Media and Performing Arts Center at Rensselaer] in Troy, New York a few years ago, I did a time-based work in which I spent about five weeks working within their theater space. I used risers and tables, different levels of staging, to put forth the final engagement: a multi-channel performance.

       The springboard for my residency proposal was René Daumal's novel *Mount Analogue* (1952), this idea of the journey: that what's inside is far more important and engaging and beneficial than reaching an end goal. I invited Sabrina Ratté, a video artist from Quebec, to come and work with me on the residency. I arranged three screens as an equilateral triangle in the back of the theater: one large screen in the center and two small ones on either side, which would essentially be a mountain range. Then I seated myself within this valley underneath the mountain range where all of the staging was dressed in African wax; it made a sculptural piece out of textiles. I was a focal point within the staging, and the screens became a focal point for the sounds. Because the sounds clustered and moved around in a non-directional manner, you couldn't anticipate where the sound would come from next.

       The idea was to create a hypnagogic state where you were surrounded and engulfed by this cloud of sound, all the while keeping your eyes focused forward. You have all of this information and all of this movement around your head at all times, which creates this dreamlike state.

       Little things. There were essentially three landscapes. There was the mountain range, which was the video projection. There was the valley in which I was seated. And I had also dressed Sabrina's table where she was doing the video work, about 30 feet away from me in the center of the room. So, you had these three landscapes that were working within the space.

AE   Was the audience set within or looking at that landscape?

RAAL   They were looking at the landscape. It's the idea of staging a different world. And when it concludes, the space either returns to what it once was, or it's been slightly manipulated into something different due to the psychic energy.

AE   I vote for the change. In thinking about this change and returning to my other example, because it's fresh in my head, Conrad wants you to work and build the performance with him when you're in the space of the performance together—an active participant rather than passive receiver. For him, it's physical in every way, which brings in the importance of duration. He says that both he and the audience are making that moment to an equal degree. So it is also political: no composer in control, rather a gathering of people together. Afterwards, what is left? It's not as if he wants us humming melodies or humming rhythms. He expects social interaction and transformation.

Now, I don't mean to imply that you don't want the audience attending to the sound or thinking with the sound, but you're not nearly as harsh or as stripped down or pared down as anything he does either. There's also no repertoire with you. There are habits of interacting with your equipment, or your voice, but there's not a harmonic or structural center. What is the role of the patterning that develops? Or maybe what I actually want to know is: What *is* after the performance, stemming from the landscape that was created?

You don't have a great deal of live recordings. Some things are released as albums, but many things aren't. How are the spaces you create successful or not successful to you as you step away from them? What is characteristic of the ones that hold you?

RAAL I don't know if I could really say; it's all circumstantial. The
      performance no longer belongs to me in a sense. I think that's
      something people need to understand about art in general,
      that it's not precious. That's a concept that I think still evades
      many people who make creative work.

AE   Evades a lot of institutions, too.
RAAL Absolutely. It's a real problem. If I make something and I
      share it with others or if I put it out in the world, it's no
      longer my own. It will always be specifically that thing that I
      made with the intentions in which I made it, but it will not be
      that thing to a multitude of people who witness it. I've given a
      lot of thought to this because people talk about ephemeral
      work. They talk about sound art. They talk about music in a
      way that is not akin to a sculptural work or a painting, and I
      don't think that difference applies. I think that each and every
      one is valid and has the potential of holding and maintaining
      the same weight as the others. But institutions still don't
      know how to deal with sound and performance properly.

AE   Museum galleries are also not made for performance or sound.
RAAL They're not made for them. These things are not considered.
      And when institutions do engage with performance-based
      work or sound-based work, it's often met with indifference.

AE   I'm not saying that I've always been above-board, but I
      would say that my feeling is that most institutions would
      never treat a painting the way they treat sound. They
      would never—pick your metaphor—have the light off, have
      the wall half-finished, or present the work upside-down,
      backwards, truncated...
RAAL There *are* technical aspects that demand a little more,
      potentially, than a painting or a sculpture would. At the same
      time, that doesn't make it lesser or unnecessarily difficult. It's
      a sad state. Institutions are getting better, but it's moving
      slowly because we're dealing with these really static and very
      stale institutions. It's the 21st century. Things need to be

163

considered in different ways at this point, and people aren't doing it because they can't figure out how to make it commodifiable.

AE   Until there's money, there's no reason to preserve.

RAAL   Right. Because they can't figure out a way to put a value on something unless it's a monetary value, which is horseshit.

AE   We are still stuck in between two extremes. You either have a museum, which is concrete, steel, and drywall with no sound baffle or wiring in the walls for equipment. (Nothing against the museum, but it was meant to be visual, and now we're trying to fill a reverberant lacking space with sound.) On the flip side, we've got spaces like EMPAC, which is completely tricked out for tech in ways you can't even imagine. So often things built there cannot easily travel elsewhere.

Either the mountain or the desert in terms of infrastructure. Coupled with this, many institutions can't think of sound or performance outside a duration that's either a 45-minute presentation that you walk away from and it's done, or a loop you don't need to concentrate on. You clap or you don't clap and also don't attend. Sound and performance is still based on a presentation model from the black box theater as opposed to a dynamic architectural model.

What would it be to make sound present, outside of thinking, "I've come to be entertained. Do I get my drink before the set? Do I get it after the set? Where's the body?" Or even worse: "Just passing through the noisy dark spaces." Scenarios where sound is treated so it just bleeds ineffectually all over space.

RAAL   And that's why, generally, the institutions and the curators that I work with either have a better understanding of those things or are willing to take the leap and figure it out. When I was commissioned to make a work for the John Michael Kohler Arts Center, I exhibited works on paper in the gallery alongside Harry Bertoia's *Sonambient* sculptures (c.1960s–1978) and Emery Blagdon's *The Healing Machine*

164

(c.1955–1986). They proposed to me to make some sort of
sonic landscape that would live within the exhibition and
people would experience sound as they were looking at the
work. I said, "Okay, well, I think the thing that's going to be
most effective is if I activate the *The Healing Machine* and
Sonambients and create a composition in which they are
speaking to each other across the room," which they had not
considered, because Blagdon's work is not necessarily meant
to be touched. It's not meant to make sound. It's up to
me to agitate these kinetic sculptures and activate them and
create work. The Kohler were very game for it, which was...

AE   Unusual.

RAAL   ...awesome. Very unusual and only possible because of
       forward-thinking curators like Karen Patterson and Shannon
       Stratton. These are people who are interested in investigating
       work and considering things in different ways: giving the
       patron of the institution a different way of looking at these
       things or understanding these things.

AE   Let's think formally about some things. I spent all day
       yesterday listening to your recordings, reading things...
       almost the whole gamut.
            In trying to pull back memories from experiences with
       your work, I kept thinking of a trajectory. You start with
       vocals that build through delay or looping, whatever sort of
       digital effect served layering. Then slowly the synthesizer
       comes to the fore, and the work changes drastically. Now,
       the voice accents more, the synthesizer weaves forward
       to form a landscape, all for a complex blend of rhythm over
       field. There's a different way that you build and abstract
       sound beyond looping and layering a recognizable core—the
       voice. Do you think of your process as abstraction?

RAAL   I think of the voice as an instrument. I thought it was
       important for me to investigate my voice in particular: as an
       instrument to create a narrative and not as a vehicle for
       language. To use the body and gesture to create these arcs

165

of sound and choirs in which a story is told. And that is very abstract—the narrative, but a narrative, nonetheless.

AE   You never sing words?

RAAL   Never.

AE   Returning to the way your sound builds: We identify voice, but at that identification we can't always tell what you're doing to your voice, although we can recognize when it isn't quite natural. We recognize transformation. We cannot have that level of identification with a synthesizer. With a synthesizer you also can't layer or loop it and make it register as transformed or abstracted. The synthesizer material is inherently more pitch transformation: an interlocking progression of patterns without an original referent. It's not about layers causing an identification of abstraction, rather, it registers abstract. Was that a conscious progression or pairing?

RAAL   I think that it was. After spending several years working specifically with the voice as a primary instrument, I wanted to have another instrument that coupled well with the voice: something that would create dynamic movement within the realm of a time-based work, within the realm of a composition, within the realm of the improvisation.

Sonically, the human voice and the synthesizer are the most closely related because you can bend sound in ways that you [would not be able to] with an acoustic instrument. You have limitations with everything, but I felt like there were certain limitations with stringed or percussive instruments that didn't provide the same possibilities. I wanted to have something where it would be unclear as to what was what, which is more to do with what is happening in that moment. The ways in which I could play with both the voice and with electricity from a synthesizer gave the highest number of variables to explore and take real time.

AE   Metaphors are always a little rickety relative to sound, but there's a sense of hovering with your early vocal stuff. There's

166

a sounding space built from a voice that rises from inside, particularly on *The Psychic Nature of Being* (2005, Kranky). When eventually the acoustic guitar comes in, it is coming out fog, out of mist. The effect is one of guitars rising, differentiated from a spectral bog of intangible voices, rather than a bold rock gesture: enter power chord. Nothing here has solid body.

More recently, as with *Kulthan* (2017, Latency), there's something increasingly liquid in the synthesized sound. Things swirl. Bubble. Things spin around. Things diverge and overtake or spill their boundaries, but it's not the same hovering. Things don't lift out or soar above and stack in the newer sounds so much. They shape, they pool, they turn back, they converge and diverge. They might be more distinct as notes but the composition is always of a piece.

RAAL Which I think is, actually, far more organic. I like thinking of the work as an organism. The amounts of variables involved with the synthesizer are far more human and less ethereal than the earlier layered looping.

AE Does that change how you think of the voice, the way you use it?

RAAL Over time it has. There are certain things that I have adhered to over time, but I think that I have been using my voice in significantly different ways, especially over the last four years or so.

AE Well, the voice sort of disappears on some of these recent recordings.

RAAL Right. Also, I like the idea of having a bed of sound; I like the idea of having a bed of voices or a choir of voices. But at the same time, I feel like I've already investigated that particular situation. I need to challenge myself. I need to be able to take myself out of a comfort zone and not have that bed of sound, and basically be naked in the room and figure it out. I like that level of unknowing, and I prefer to engage with myself and my work in a way that I may find something that I have not considered before and can investigate wholeheartedly.

167

AE   I wonder if I can ask one question in two ways: I want to ask about breath. Of course, breath is important; you can't sing without breathing. I want to know what you have thought about breath, in this way, but also in the sense of *breadth*: making space to allow something different to enter. Because you're not phrasing; you're not thinking about having enough wind to finish the lyrical line. In this, I'm thinking of singers like Caetano Veloso, who has an amazing ability to draw a line out. You listen to how long he can sing before he breaks, and you feel, "This is a man that's holding a power." But you're not singing words, so you are not extending lines; you are building patterns. How are you conscious of breath?

RAAL Early on, specifically building the durational works and the choirs of myself, I would do these really long, drawn-out throws that would not waver, and I would hold the note for however long and let that dissipate—then hold it again and again. And then maybe step up a third and then maybe open up my voice to make it reedier and put a flourish here. The breathing would come in the moment. Once I had established a baseline, I would work around that. It's always about establishing the first brush stroke: how to build around that and how to strip it away?

      As time went on, I started thinking a lot more about the body and how I held the body. Within a performance my body would move sort of unconsciously. Someone would ask me about it later, and I would say, "I don't know what you're talking about. I don't realize how I'm holding my hands or how I've arched my back or these sorts of things." Because it was more about trance: letting go and becoming lost. But there was still a bit of consciousness in there that would move around and initiate movements with the voice.

      Slowly but surely, I was able to figure out a way to levitate, if you will, while remaining in the driver's seat... at times letting go of the wheel and seeing where the vehicle goes. But I've become more conscious of these intentional moves and turns. So—with the voice and with breath and within the breadth of my work—I feel that I've progressed in a way that

I've been able to go from a complete letting-go to holding onto the reins in a way that anomalies introduce themselves without needing to course-correct. That's huge: letting a mistake remain without trying to right the ship, whether slight or severe.

AE   Now you're trying to find this space performatively or conceptually, and not necessarily physically. It's more architecture. If I take this and set it within what you said about improvisation and trying to build a sound space, your work is less about the dichotomy between having to be in control or letting go, and more about making architecture happen as a performance: architecture forming as a resonant room.

RAAL   I'm in the mode of consistently exploring that, because I think there's a lot of room to move. Every time the dice are rolled, a different number comes up.

AE   In that, let's think about technology. Are machines important to you? You came from the voice; it is the original instrument, right? But obviously other things are important to you as well... the fabric under your equipment and the setting up of the synthesizer. I'm trying to ask if technology is also a space? Is this a machine space?

RAAL   No. Technology is interesting for me, but ultimately not necessary. I've done performances that were completely a capella. I remember specifically doing a performance where the idea was no PA. I was singing into the air, and I had two cymbals and a bow. I was creating a space dealing more with silence, with things falling away.

    The technology is only important because with the synthesizer there are so many variables involved. I need quite a long time to even investigate the modules inside the instrument that I currently have. There are plentiful ways to move inside over and over and over again. Ever since I was a child I was interested in synthesizers.

AE   What brought you to them?

RAAL   The first synthesizer record I heard was *Switched-On Bach*
(Columbia Records, 1968) by Wendy Carlos. I just really
enjoyed the sound. As I got older and understood the
concepts more, I was fascinated that the first modular
synthesizer was made to be an instrument for future music.
That's something that makes a lot of sense to me because
I have no issue with tradition, and yet I have every issue with
relying solely on tradition.

I was a punk kid. I started playing music because I was
a punk. And very quickly I started to get a lot weirder and
do stranger things. I was also listening to a lot of jazz and
classical. I was listening to a lot of left-field forms. From
Diamanda Galás to Steve Reich to Bad Brains...

AE   From there, what gave you the confidence for the big jump
out of standard music group conventions? Everyone starts in
a band. In my mind, a punk band, a country band, a big band,
or an orchestra aren't that different or unusual in the social
dynamic. You're on stage with others in tandem. But that's
very different from, "I'm going to go onstage a capella: just
my voice. This risk—this is my own."

RAAL   That's an interesting question. I don't know if I have an
answer for that. I don't know if there was necessarily a
defining point. I do remember the first piece of music that I
was really struck by, which was the Neptune movement in
Gustav Holst's *Planets* (1914–1916). It is really whimsical and
melancholy at the same time. There was something about
that. You have, of course, "Mars," which John Williams
essentially ripped off to make the *Star Wars* theme, but then
you have these more delicate, fragile movements within
"Neptune." That was something that really spoke to me and
that I recall from a very young age.

Also, when I was 17 years old, I helped put on a Caspar
Brötzmann Massaker show in Kansas City, where I'm from.
That was a crazy turning point for me, because the sound of
the trio was creating this feeling. I thought plaster was falling
off the ceiling because I felt things hitting my shoulders and

the top of my head. Then I realized that it was just my nerve endings tingling because the band was hitting these very specific frequencies. That shattered my mind.

AE   That's a good one.... In listening to a lot of your recordings yesterday, I was drawn to reread Louis Chude-Sokei's essay *Dr. Satan's Echo Chamber* (2013). I started thinking about the echo chamber, as he calls it, and technological space— hence my earlier question about technology. Chude-Sokei claims that dub takes a music or song for granted and takes recording for granted and takes technology for granted in that it is largely processing and manipulating between these things rather than generating something new. But what that processing does is create a new political, social, and sound space from the echo generated by manipulating song, recording, and technology. Echo space is important because echo keeps you triangulated—bouncing—between sound, projection, reception, and understanding: Receiving and projecting toggle together. More importantly, each is registered. Producing rather than authoring.

When you talk about memory in your work—and I wonder how to register memory as a listener—I started thinking about echo. Pattern is increasingly important to your music. And the pace of your pattern often makes a space where the listener can register the technology responding to or transforming, over which you weave or interject your voice. Do they reverberate against one another internally? Do they respond? What is drawn to echo?

RAAL I think it's a combination. There are ways in which there's a very understandable change within the length of the form, and then there are other times where the motifs cycle back and sort of clatter around and gain momentum inside of that chamber as the duration continues.

AE   With this echoing around we talk about things returning, we talk memory, we talk psychic space, we talk change from what was. You said early on that you are thinking through narrative. And I've also been thinking a lot about narrative in music. Usually when we talk about experimental music we talk about a progression of abstraction. John Cage extending the expansion of form in Schoenberg or techno building from minimalism, which in turn extended and rewired serialism. We're always articulating further and further abstractions. People never talk about narrative, in and as narrative, as possibly being experimental for music. Narrative is thought of as regressive: pop songs, opera, etc. Think about many reactions to Robert Ashley, even from creative music heads...

RAAL   ...He's absolutely experimental.

AE   Yeah. But given that he offers stories, and the sounds setting these stories are often slightly cocktail-y in tone, he still gets brushed to the side. People think it is corny and deemphasize what can be done with a voice speaking, with a monologue, and with the setting of a person's voice in a political landscape. But you don't tell stories or monologue; your sound is rather abstract. So what is narrative for you?

RAAL   A lot of my work is site-specific. I do consider the invitation to do the work. The narrative comes through in this idea of moments. On a basic level, having conversations with people after performances where they will tell me, "Okay, I understood this to be this, and took me here," or, "I thought about this within the duration of the work." That's important to me because I've begun to cultivate this technique in which I am imparting a bit of myself to others and they interpret or understand that.

AE   Is there a narrative center to your performances, then?
RAAL   I am the center.

AE   You're not going to give up that focal position. It's not fully a collaborative making?
RAAL   No.

AE   There's something solipsistic about the performance?

172

RAAL   Absolutely.

AE   Is there a political or social charge? Something for wanting
      that pattern, that reverberation, that narration of memory in
      front of people?
RAAL   Yeah. Ultimately for me, it's most important that others
      understand this concept of cultivation of technique and
      development of tradition outside of what they already know.

AE   So it's dispersal of approach?
RAAL   Exactly. Dispersal is a good way of thinking about it.

AE   Are there ghosts in the music?
RAAL   That's without question.

AE   Now that you've got decades of performance under your belt,
      are there ghosts that return frequently?
RAAL   Absolutely. There are memories that manifest themselves in
      the middle of performance, and that may push my physical
      body in one way or the arc of the performance in one way.

AE   If we're then heading out with memory grounded by narrative
      and ghosts, we're not heading out like an airplane heads
      out. We're heading via a different kind of out. We're heading
      out by grounding here, by being present and rebuilding where
      we are. Not moving to another territory to plant our flag.
RAAL   I look at sound as something that's tangible. Not necessarily
      the physicality of sound, but the emotional response that you
      have to the work that's put in front of you. Within that
      landscape that's built up over the performance time or
      recording, there will be a memory, which is an approximation
      of the event, not the actuality. Each individual will recall
      either fondly or indifferently or pessimistically. They have a
      thing. It's fascinating that memory is an approximation.

Tarek Atoui, Feedbacking

Ida Soulard

Tarek Atoui rarely works on stage and does not produce records, nor any other fixed forms of composition. Rather, he "works with sound in various spaces, whether in galleries or museum halls or outdoor setting" and constructs, as he said in a 2018 interview with Diana Nguyen on Marfa Public Radio, an "experiential way of listening to a concert of musical performances" that does not only "involves the ears as a way of listening, but also involves the eyes, the body, the sense of touch." These physical sound experiments rely on an expanded practice of composition. For *Marfa Sounding*, Atoui created two live performances: at Saint George Hall, a concert venue that opens to the outside, and at Vizcaino Park, an open-air amphitheater and community park. These two performances were preceded by a series of workshops open to all members of the Marfa community as well as to international art students in residence at Fieldwork Marfa. This essay follows a conversation with Tarek Atoui held in Paris in June 2018 where we discussed his practice of composition, work methods, modes of collaboration and music as an experimental space for constructing new forms of knowledge.

COMPOSITION AS FEEDBACK

In 2016, two years before Atoui's Marfa performances, *Marfa Sounding* hosted American composer Alvin Lucier. Among other works, he performed at the Crowley Theater his iconic sound piece, *I Am Sitting in a Room* (1969). The score reads as follows:

> I am sitting in a room different from the one you are
> in now. I am recording the sound of my speaking voice
> and I am going to play it back into the room again
> and again until the resonant frequencies of the room
> reinforce themselves so that any semblance of my
> speech, with perhaps the exception of rhythm, is
> destroyed. What you will hear, then, are the natural
> resonant frequencies of the room articulated by speech.
> I regard this activity not so much as a demonstration
> of a physical fact, but more as a way to smooth out any
> irregularities my speech might have.

I Am Sitting in a Room can be described as a form of feedback loop. Lucier's voice is recorded and played back with its natural reverb in a repetitive pattern, slowly dissolving the voice within the reverberation of the space. This controlled feedback (recorded voice—amplification—speakers) opens to the sonic expression of the theater itself and immerses the audience in their material and acoustic environment. This progressive emergence of the background as figure has a long-standing history in both sound and visual art.

Such attempts at foregrounding the material properties of the background using feedback started in the late 1960s and early '70s (under the influence of the work of composers such as David Tudor or John Cage). With the emergence of new audio and video recording technologies and the influence of Cybernetics, feedback became an increasingly privileged figure in art: in music with Robert Ashley's tape music *The Wolfman* (1964), which uses feedback as a main source for composition; the production of cybersonic devices by the Sonic Arts Union (Gordon Mumma, David Behrman, Robert Ashley, and Alvin Lucier, initiated in 1966) that manipulate the acoustic properties of a space by playing in interaction with those properties; Steve Reich's phasing feedback tones of *Pendulum* (1968); and in Max Neuhaus's early works with electroacoustic feedback like *Fontana Mix Feed* (1968). The same is true for the visual arts with works such as the video performance *Boomerang* (1974) by Nancy Holt and Richard Serra, Vito Acconci's video performance *Centers* (1971), or the use of closed physical systems in Hans Haacke's sculptures such as *Condensation Cube* (1965), to name just a few.

Critic Rosalind Krauss theorizes feedback as a constitutive figure of postmodernity in her 1976 *October* essay, *Video: The Aesthetics of Narcissism*. In this text, Krauss asserts that the medium of video (and hence the postmodern condition) is Narcissism, folding back the materiality of the medium onto a psychological condition. Krauss starts with an analysis of *Centers* by Acconci. The closed circuit between Acconci pointing at the center of a TV screen while looking at himself pointing at the center of the TV screen creates a feedback loop where the "projection and the

176

reception of an image" coincide, thus blurring the boundaries between input and output, subject and object. Krauss continues with Serra and Holt's *Boomerang* video piece, in which Holt is describing her situation: talking and hearing her voice echoing back with a 1-second delay. She says the situation is "like a mirror-reflection...so that I am surrounded by me and my mind surrounds me...there is no escape." The name Krauss gives to this feeling of self-entrapment (or "self-encapsulation") expressed by Holt is the "prison of the collapsed present" (inaugural issue of *October*, Spring 1976). The feedback severs us both from past and future to focus on a new form of "now," an exhausted present that crosses out all possibilities for any futurity. Tautology may have been a formal equivalent of feedback for the visual arts: a dynamic motif of time-space organization and the expression of a generalized feeling of entrapment where the only degree of freedom seems to lay in the infra-space produced by the loop and its delay, a mirror-like movement, the space of a trap. In the feedback, as theorized by Krauss, the physical and material conditions of its emergence become less important than the effects produced and the way such effects affect the subject—i.e., their psychological impact. Feedback's importance as a postmodern figure is because of the specific time-space it both contains and produces: the folding back onto a form of "now" severed from any kind of futurity.

But feedback (and there are many kinds) is also a process, and its uses in music (left aside in Krauss's theory) help open and further her definition of it. Its early use in electronic sound allowed for a number of new directions in experimental music: for "duration that exceeds the conventional instrumental gestures, it's self-sustaining-ness," as Matthieu Saladin discusses (*Organised Sound*, 22, Aug. 2017); for the progressive withdrawal of the performer or its connection with the machine; for the foregrounding of background noises and a focus on the specific space and architecture where the music is played; for the opening of multiple perspectives on sound (the dispersion of the center); and for the opening on sound as a tridimensional object. Space became—through the environmental compositions of Lucier, Reich, and Neuhaus—a major component in music production: space as transforming the sound, the sound as producing space, and the presence and movement of the audience impacting the overall production of the sound-space connection. The multiple uses of feedback in music productions of the 1960s and '70s, by taking into account their immediate environment and opening to the potentialities of the background, leave aside the realm of the psychological to the architectural, the environmental, and a wider feedback gesture that goes from the musician/performer to the site of the performance and back.

WORKS AND PROCESS (2013–2018)

Tarek Atoui's work is in direct line with this legacy: a music that takes into account the specificity of a space or site (environmental music) and foregrounds the background on which it unfolds; a practice of composition that uses feedback processes as a motif of organization; and performances that stress their impact on both performers and audience. But in a similar movement to what happened in the visual arts with the shifting notion of site-specificity (the background that becomes foregrounded as figure) since the mid-1960s, as well as the progressive expansion of that background to spheres other than the purely material and literal specificities of a site (to the social, political, geological), Atoui's sound art considerably expands the understanding of what a site (the background) is, as well as how to intervene in it. His compositional work is a long durational process spread across years and various locations. It relies on four major elements: inquiry, collaboration, the production of new instruments, and the synthetic weaving of those three processes; each feeding (or feedbacking) upon the others by relaunching new projects and synthetic propositions. The feedback with which Atoui works produces a radically different dynamic than the one manipulated by sound artists in the 1960s and '70s.

The Reverse Collection, initiated in 2013 in the ethnographic storage vault of the Dahlem Museum in Berlin, consists of a series of new instruments created through a "reverse" process. Atoui began his inquiry by investigating instruments stored in the museum's vault and, over the course of eight months, invited a

178

group of eighteen experimental musicians (percussion, wind, and strings) to improvise on a select number of these instruments. Some musicians had to play upon ladders in the vault in order not to move the most fragile elements from their conservation spaces. The product of this first layer, called the *Dahlem Session*, was a sound library made of recordings of the solo performances from the storage vault. These recordings were at a later stage mixed and arranged by Atoui to produce a new score to be improvised upon live by the same musicians at the 2014 Berlin Biennale.

For the second layer of the project, titled *The Reverse Sessions*, Atoui gave the recordings of those solo performances (with no other information, severing the sound from its socio-cultural and historical context) to instrument makers and asked them to build new instruments that would be able to replicate the sounds as they heard and understood them. Eight instruments were consequently produced and then activated at kurimanzutto gallery in Mexico in 2014.

The third layer took place in 2016 in London at the Tate Modern where the instruments were exhibited and recurrently activated by performers (amateurs and professionals) during the time of the exhibition. Atoui made another series of recordings from these live performances that were then arranged and transformed into a multichannel, evolving sound piece played continuously over the course of the exhibition.

The multi-step processes of *The Reverse Collection/The Reverse Sessions* is representative of Atoui's compositional method at large: a long durational process where each layer builds up and feeds back into the following, creating a positive feedback loop from inquiry to live performance and from recordings to the production of new instruments that in turn produce new live performances opening to expanded fields of inquiry, and so on.

WITHIN is another multifaceted project initiated in 2012, and which includes a series of concerts and live performances, exhibitions, workshops, production of instruments and software, sonic exercises, sound library, and program of videos and films documenting the project. The inquiry started after a residency at the Sharjah Art Foundation in 2008—an investigation into the

179

physicality of sound and its tactile qualities—and was augmented through a collaboration with the curatorial and production platform *Council* led by Sandra Terdjman and Gregory Castera (TACET, 2013), which explores "the diversity of listening modes" in the context of the Sharjah Art Foundation. TACET's inquiry was, at the time, central in Atoui's concerns. In 2012, with the Sharjah Art Foundation, Atoui presented a project entitled *Below 160*, which primarily used bass and sub-bass frequencies and was first performed in front of a hearing audience and then played for students of the Al Amal School for the Deaf. Atoui also invited various international percussionists (the drum being an instrument that can be heard and felt), including Brian Chippendale, Susie Ibarra, and YoshimiO, to perform in strategic public locations throughout the city (rooftops, squares, etc.). In the context of TACET, and following a series of private and public workshops with students from the Al Amal school, researchers, sound artists, theoreticians, translators, curators, and educators, Atoui had the idea for WITHIN: a new instrumentarium that "tackles the ways in which deafness can influence our understanding of sound performance, its space and its instrumentation" (Bergen Assembly, 2016). As a result of the overall process of inquiry, residency, live performance, and workshop, Atoui produced nine new instruments with visual or tactile qualities able to address both hearing and deaf audiences.

Among those instruments, all of which were shown and performed together for the first time at the 2016 Bergen Assembly of which Atoui was artistic director, was the *0.9* brought to Marfa two years later. Conceived in collaboration with UC Berkeley Associate Professor Greg Niemeyer, Perrin Meyer of the sound company Meyer Sound, and Jeffrey Lubow from the Center for New Media at UC Berkeley, the *0.9* is a group of nine subwoofers producing ultra-low frequency electronic sounds (8 to 120hz), divided into three units, and each topped by a wooden platform on which a performer stands. An infrared sensor placed upon a mic-stand detects hand and finger movements, inspired by sign language, which command the intensity and movement of the ultra-low frequency. These sounds can be both heard and felt by standing barefoot on the wooden platform. "I call it a subsonic theremin. You can use gestures with your fingers and palms to create unique subsonic sound patterns with a subtle but compelling psychoacoustic effect," explains Atoui an online brochure published in 2016 by Bergen Assembly. The instrument was first performed at Mills College and Hearst Memorial Mining at UC Berkeley in 2015 after three weeks of co-teaching with Niemeyer and months of developing sketches for the new instrument. The project was later pursued in 2016 at EMPAC, an Experimental Media and Performing Arts Center in Troy, New York, in collaboration with composer and musician Pauline Oliveros and Rensselaer Polytechnic Institute students.

During Atoui's first public concert of *Marfa Sounding*, at Saint George Hall, an event space located next to the train tracks, the *0.9* was played by six volunteers who trained during two workshop sessions. They were accompanied by four professional musicians (Atoui included) who improvised, each with their own instruments, upon the vibrations produced by the *0.9*. The physicality of the sound could be experienced by leaning on walls and feeling with your body, through the metal architecture of the space, the sonic vibrations of the multi-part instrument.

During *Marfa Sounding*, *0.9* cohabitated with another instrument: two *Sound Boxes* extracted from another project, *I/E Elefsis*, which in turn followed an invitation to work in Elefsina, a post-industrial city on the outskirts of Athens, Greece for the Aisxylia Festival in 2015. *I/E Elefsis* consists again of a multifaceted project made of a sound-proof shipping container that functioned as a collective instrument and which contained the following: field recordings made by the renowned field recordist Chris Watson (and founder of the Sheffield group Cabaret Voltaire) taken at three sites in Elefsina (ancient ruins, an industrial port, and an abandoned oil factory); and images of these recordings processed by French photographer Alexandre Guirkinger.

In Elefsina, *I/E* functioned "as an information center for the exhibition, as a point of reference, as a listening station, and as a performance platform" ("I/E Elefsis", 2015, Locus Athens). Atoui processed the field recordings and produced a composition upon

which he invited six Greek musicians to improvise. He then pushed
this project further by developing a minimalist wooden box that
allowed him to open up new ways of working with concrete sounds
and field recordings. Atoui then reproduced the same process
in other harbors (Singapore, Abu Dhabi, and Porto), each time
producing new boxes that together develop the combinatory
possibilities of a modular synthesizer. While the Athens box
brought to Marfa has an acoustic feel, in Abu Dhabi's, the concrete
sounds undergo a spectral morphing and Singapore's opens to
a work with resonance, distortion, and wave banding. "The
environment is not just sound material or a sound source—its
acoustics and social dynamics, for example, can inform composition
and inspire new ways to perform and collaborate," says Atoui.
These specificities depend on the sonic memory the artist keeps
of each visited place.

COLLABORATION AND IMPROVISATION

Atoui's practice relies on invitations to an international network
of musicians, artists, engineers, researchers, and amateurs who
collaborate on both his music and the construction of new
instruments. For *Marfa Sounding,* he invited three professional
musicians, all US-based, two of whom were regular collaborators
of his (Jad Atoui—Tarek's brother—and Robert Aiki Aubrey Lowe)
and one, Jeanie Aprille Tang aka Amma Ateria, with whom he was
working for the first time. Before selecting the performers, Atoui
spends hours carefully listening to their musical work in order
to understand their sonic identities. The performers are also
selected by their capacity to adapt, lean into the background, be
flexible, and quickly process a vast amount of information; in short,
great improvisers with a strong individual sonic identity.

Atoui then produces a structure for improvisation: a set of
constraints within which performers can work. A score gives
the timing of the overall performance and sets both collective play
and individual soloing. In the context of the *Marfa Sounding*
performances, Atoui worked through layers: tracks of concrete sound
coming out from Athens *Sound Box* and movements of foregrounding
and backgrounding of the sounds of the invited musicians were all

injected into the *0.9,* which became not only an instrument to be played but also a tool for amplification. The set of constraints that Atoui produces—within which controlled hazard and unpredictability can take place—is strong and would be "too hard on an acoustic performer," says Atoui. These constraints are also what make each performance unique. Atoui produces the situation, but what happens within that situation can never be replicated.

Collaboration, transmission, and pedagogy are a crucial part of Atoui's practice. When the *0.9* was completed at Berkeley in 2015, performers included composer and musician James Fei (who also participated in *Marfa Sounding* 2016), UC Berkeley students, and other performers both professional and amateur. In Marfa, Atoui's residency started with a series of workshops at Marfa High School as well as with two open "rehearsals" held on the performances venue sites of Vizcaino Park and Saint George Hall, open to all members of (or visitors to) the community. The first rehearsal functioned as an introduction to both analog and digital technologies used in improvisation, Tarek's understanding of sound production, and the function and dynamic of both his and Jad's instruments. The second rehearsal focused on the two instruments to be used in the live performance: *0.9* and the *Sound Boxes.* In this second gathering, Atoui gave participants the opportunity to experiment and play the *0.9* instrument. Following this exchange, six of the workshop participants volunteered to train further in order to perform during the two public concerts.

An educator himself, this systematic work with amateurs from all ages and backgrounds highlights how Atoui sees the function of music in his work as a tool to be used by professionals and non-specialists alike. "My aim is to see these instruments and their repertoire enter a music school or an educational institution that intends to set up a music program for Deaf and hearing people," explains Atoui, who hopes that the experiments and creative methodologies he develops will have a direct and immediate empowering impact on communities. Relying on co-operation—the sharing of competences, reciprocity, and mutual recognition—Atoui's pieces are always the result of a strong net of collaborations and complex collective signatures. The makers developing the prototype-instruments are then owner of the design and free to develop them for their own purposes. Students become collaborators in their own right, bringing both ideas and materials. What Atoui is creating is a new genre of music school, dispersed both geographically and in time; where new instruments are built through sessions of collective and individual experimentations opening to an expanded understanding of what hearing and music are and can be.

The emphasis placed on transmission is also one of the reasons why, against the current trend towards sound miniaturization, Atoui builds instruments at the scale of a human body. The monumental presence of the *0.9* or the minimalist physicality of the *Sound Boxes* attest to Atoui's interest in performance, the body, and gestural propositions. This allows both for the performer to physically interact with the instrument—to reinject the human body in electronic practices (and use the body as an instrument)—as well as for the mostly non-specialist audience to follow and understand visually, through gestural performance, the function of the instrument and the unfolding of the sound piece. In this way, the displacement of *0.9* in the context of Marfa is highly significative of his overall practice: a work within chapters where an instrument made for a specific project (an inquiry on deaf culture and its consequences for sound and hearing practices) evolves and continues to be tested through subsequent institutional invitations, relying on a network of collaborators with different kinds of competences (instrument makers, educators, software engineers, amateurs, composers, sound companies, etc.). Each test or new performance opens potentialities for the instruments and helps to expand knowledge of perception, the body, the ear, the tactile qualities of sound, and sonic materiality through practice.

THE MARFA EXPERIENCE: A NEW PHASE
If Atoui's work has appealed so widely to audiences in the globalized contemporary art world, it may be because of its focus on experience, live performance, the sculptural quality of the instruments, and the idea that musical quality matters less than its potential to affect the audience and produce embodied thinking.

The final *Marfa Sounding* performance offered such an experience.

At Vizcaino Park—a popular location where teenagers go cruising, local gatherings are organized, and barbecue celebrations are held on summer days—Atoui's performance started at dusk and lasted until nightfall. In selecting familiar spaces used by Marfa's multiple communities, Atoui's intention was to recast known locations and everyday architectures by allowing them to be experienced in a new way through sound. On the concrete floor, against an unbounded view of the desert, stood the three-part *0.9* instrument and the invited musicians. They were dispersed in space, forming a circle within which the audience was lying and sitting, wandering sometimes from one performer to the next. The desert has an acoustic quality impossible to saturate despite the *0.9* instrument operating at full power, as both instrument and surface for amplification. Six amateur performers took shifts upon the *0.9*, and the three professional musicians (Jad Atoui, Amma Ateria, and Robert Aiki Aubrey Lowe) formed the rest of the circle. Tarek Atoui acted as both performer and master of ceremony.

Three layers of different sonic quality weave through the performance: the telluric sound of the *0.9* instrument's low frequency; the oneiric presence of concrete sounds from the Athens and Abu Dhabi harbors opening to a mental projection into foreign spaces; and the lyrical presence of the performers—the play of tension and release of eruptive atmospheres synthetically reproduced by Ateria, the eerie voice and analog modular system of Lowe, and Jad Atoui's subtle improvisations on his analog machine. The experience was one of inclusiveness, even though the absence of focal point (the dispersion of musicians and instruments in space) did not allow for a common encounter, but rather for a multi-perspectival, individualized experience within a collective hearing situation. Begun under a dimming summer sky, the performance went through a series of intense color variations as the celestial vault turned blue, orange, and bright pink, before concluding under a quasi-full moon. At the end, musicians and audience members remained still for a few moments, the music giving way to the gradual rise of cricket chirping, as if on cue.

At Vizcaino Park, the performance worked as a hypnotic visual
and sonic experiment while simultaneously demanding an acute
hearing presence from the audience.

In Marfa, Atoui initiated a new phase in his practice, which is
planned to last for at least two years: a re-synthesis of existing
projects taken out of their initial framework and recombined in
new kinds of performances. Atoui takes out ideas—semantic or
sonic output—from the instruments in order to reconfigure them in
new propositions. For example, the *0.9* instrument is composed
of two major ideas that Atoui is currently working on separately:
sign language, on one hand, and a play with architecture via the
displacement of low frequencies in space, on the other. Both of
these ideas may give birth to new instruments. *The Reverse
Collection* is currently being re-synthesized in an organ that will
function as a mechanical modular synthesizer played by twelve
people: half of the instruments are being built for non-hearing
audiences and performers (with the help of a drawing interface)
and the other half for hearing performers, mixing ideas from *The
Reverse Collection* and WITHIN through the fabrication of a new
instrument. *Glitter Beats and Wild Synths / The Wave*, presented at
the Okayama Triennale in 2019, is an orchestral composition with
nine instruments taken out of WITHIN, *The Reverse Collection*,
some new productions, and all recombined in a fixed compositional
loop of 34 minutes. *The Wave* may also be Atoui's most narrative
piece to date, where the slow deep breath of the Horns of Putin,
like a merciless tide, attempts three times to overflow all the other
instruments therefore trying to resist their own forced,
programmed disappearance. "Computer programming lead me to
think in a modular way and to think about composition as the sum
of independent modules that can come together through the
performance," says Tarek. This extended modular approach (new
instrument design, sound textures, and body relations) opens to
an expansive field of non-reproducible combinatorial possibilities,
due to the high sensitivity of the parameters involved.

Composition, in Atoui's practice, increasingly works through
intertwining layers: inquiry, recordings, construction of
instruments, improvisation in live performances and installations,

and experiments or "test sessions" in various contexts. These layers
produce a first positive feedback loop, which then crystallizes
and becomes one module like *The Reverse Collection* or WITHIN;
this module then becomes one element for a new composition.
Each module can be fragmented in sub-elements that become
starting components for a new compositional loop, in other words,
they can be resynthesized. In Atoui's practice, there are no clear
cuts—no beginnings or endings—but rather a series of loops,
modular processes, and synthetic movements. This double
movement consists in, first, grounding the music within a specific
site that possess a specific set of constraints, and then, uprooting
it to be able to use it as one component in a synthesizer: this
branching works at every scale, from a single composition to his
overall working method. Contrary to Krauss's understanding
of feedback, here identities and specificities are created through
the feedback process (and not already fixed and altered by the
feedbacking process, i.e., Narcissism) and the strength of Atoui's
method is to function both at the level of music and at the social
level, with specific communities (i.e., as a social synthesizer).

While performers from the 1960s and '70s focused primarily
on the physical conditions (reverb, noises coming from the
audience, etc.) of the chosen site or architecture to express or
foreground those "background" parameters as sonic tools, Atoui
expands the number of parameters involved. The site he focuses on
is always simultaneously specific and generic. He takes into account
the multiple histories, social concerns, and specific bodies of each
singular space while working through and across various
geographies, sites, and scales. Each of his specific works, produced
for a specific site, becomes one module for a broader construction
that can then be uprooted from its event of creation or instantiation,
fabricating a new synthetic composition.

CONTRIBUTORS

ANDREW ABRAHAMS

Founder and president of Open Eye Pictures, Andrew Abrahams is a multi-award-winning, Oscar-shortlisted, and Emmy-nominated maker of creative nonfiction films. He is also a skilled cinematographer and photographer. After enrolling in the Medill School of Journalism, Andrew received a BA in Cultural Anthropology from Northwestern University and an MA in Visual Anthropology from the University of Southern California, where he also studied at the School of Cinema. Andrew's approach emphasizes visual imagery as a way to bridge disparate parts, peoples, and ideas. While his work takes on controversial themes, he uses the filmmaking process as an opportunity to encourage compassion and action. In addition to making films, Andrew teaches unique film and photo workshops, including *Intimacy & Exposure: The Alchemy of Photography* at the renowned Esalen Institute.

CLAIRE AMIOT

Claire Amiot lives and works between Nantes and Finistère. She was part of the DUST (Desert Unit for Speculative Territories) education program in 2018, where she performed in Tarek Atoui's series of concerts. She works with a diversity of materials, from painted textiles to electronic music. She graduated from Beaux-Arts Nantes Saint-Nazaire in 2019. She is co-founder of ZUT, an artist-run space located in Brittany, France (Morbihan). She has presented her work in several exhibitions in France and the US.

AMMA ATERIA

Amma Ateria (Jeanie-Aprille Tang) is an electroacoustic composer, improviser, and sound artist born in Hong Kong, based in California. Her work explores themes in the coexistence of polarity and psychoacoustics with a focus in equal-loudness contour. With an immediacy of tension and release, her performances navigate between oppositions through stark transitions, turning deafening noise into a meditative stance. Through cross-modal synesthetic influences from the contemporary moment, the notion of externalizing resonances acts as a form of questioning, of boundaries, and the brinks of breakage in the sonic spectrum. With memories of condensed cities, she gravitates to frequencies of close-range airplanes, polyrhythmic occurrences, inaudible conversations, out-of-body experiences, sustained harmonics intersected with musique concrète, distorted speech, and synthesized speed of air.

JAD ATOUI

Jad Atoui is a music composer, sound designer, and electronic sound experimentalist. Using biosensors, field recordings, and analog gears, he composes and performs experimental electronic music. Along with Ivan Marazzi, he spearheaded the *Biosonics* project in 2015, in order to incorporate the bio-sonification of behaviors as a compositional tool. The project was published in John Zorn's book *Arcana XVIII: musicians on music* (2017) and premiered at The National Sawdust (New York) as part of Zorn's Stone Commissioning Series (2017). He has also worked with musicians such as Laurie Anderson, John Zorn, Chuck Bettis, Bill Frisell, Michael Coltun, Marc Ribot, Sharif Sehnaoui, and Elliott Sharp.

TAREK ATOUI

Tarek Atoui is an artist and composer, working within the realm of sound. His practice revolves around performances that develop from extensive research into music history and tradition, and explores new methods of collaboration and production. At the core of his work is an ongoing reflection on the notion of instrument and how it overlaps with composing and performing. Atoui's use of sound challenges and expands our established ways of understanding and experiencing this medium. Atoui has presented his work internationally at the Sydney Biennale (2020); Okayama Art Summit (2019); Sharjah Biennial in the United Arab Emirates (2009 and 2013); dOCUMENTA 13 in Kassel, Germany (2012); 8th Berlin Biennial (2014); Tate Modern, London (2016); CCA NTU, Singapore (2017); Garage Moscow (2018); 58th International Art Exhibition of la Biennale di Venezia (2019); and at the Okayama Art Summit 2019. He was co-artistic director of STEIM studios in 2007 and the Bergen Assembly (Norway) in 2016.

JENNIFER BURRIS

Jennifer Burris is a curator and writer based in Bogotá, Colombia. She has organized solo and group exhibitions at the Museo de Arte Moderno, Bogotá; Brooklyn Museum, New York; Institute of Contemporary Art, Philadelphia; and Haverford College, Pennsylvania. As a writer she has contributed to publications including *The Journal of Aesthetics and Art Criticism*, *Studies in French Cinema*, *Bomb*, *Revista Código*, *Afterall*, and *frieze*, as well as multiple artist monographs. From 2018-2020, she was an Assistant Professor at Nanyang Technological University in Singapore where she was part of the founding faculty for the first graduate program in Curatorial Practice and Museum Studies in Southeast Asia.

JACQUELINE CAUX

With a background in psychoanalysis, Jacqueline Caux is a filmmaker and writer whose work focuses on the experimental music, dance, and art communities of the 1960s and '70s. She has realized several documentaries and short experimental films, which have been selected for many festivals in both France and abroad. As a writer, she has published books of interviews and is a contributor to the French art magazine *art press*. Caux has also organized new music festivals and realized "horspiels" for Radio France - France Culture.

MARIA CHÁVEZ

Born in Lima, Peru and based in NYC, Maria Chávez is best known as an abstract turntablist, sound artist and DJ. Coincidence, chance, and failures are themes that unite her book objects, sound sculptures, installations, and other works with her improvised solo turntable performance practice. Maria is currently on the cover of the textbook on the history of experimental and electronic music from Routledge and is a David Tudor and Robert Rauschenberg Arts Fellow. Her large-scale sound & multi-media installations along with other sound works have been shown at the Getty Museum, the JUDD Foundation, Haus Fur Elektronische Kunste Basel, Documenta 14 in Kassel, Germany, and more. She was a research fellow for Goldsmiths University from 2015–17 and is currently an Artist in Residence with EMPAC @ RPI until 2021. Maria is on a medical sabbatical due to receiving brain surgery in February 2019 to cure a rare brain disorder. She hopes to return to performing for the public in 2022-23. She appreciates everyone's patience and compassion.

CHARLES CURTIS

Charles Curtis performs a unique repertoire of major solo works created expressly for him by La Monte Young and Marian Zazeela, Alvin Lucier, Éliane Radigue, Christian Wolff, Tashi Wada, and Alison Knowles, rarely-heard compositions by Terry Jennings and Richard Maxfield, and works by Cardew, Feldman, and Cage. A former faculty member at Princeton University, and for eleven years the first solo cellist of the NDR Symphony Orchestra in Hamburg, Curtis is now Professor of Contemporary

Music Performance at the University of California, San Diego and tours and records internationally. He continues to perform and record the traditional repertoire for cello, both as soloist and as artistic director of the chamber music project Camera Lucida.

ERIK DELUCA

Erik DeLuca is an artist and musician from Florida. He has lectured, performed, and exhibited at a variety of places including MASS MoCA, Emily Carr University of Art + Design, Art Basel (Miami), School of the Arts Institute Chicago, The Contemporary Austin, The Living Art Museum in Iceland, Columbia School of the Arts, Skowhegan School for Painting and Sculpture, CalArts, Bemis Center for Contemporary Arts, Issue Project Room, Fieldwork Marfa, Danspace Project at St Mark's Church, and Yale University School of Art. He received a PhD in Music Composition from the University of Virginia, was a lecturer at the Iceland University of the Arts (2016–18), and is currently Visiting Assistant Professor of Music and Multimedia at Brown University.

JD DIFABBIO

JD DiFabbio is an independent development advisor, grant writer, and nonprofit program producer. Based in Marfa, Texas since 2005, she previously served as Deputy Director of Marfa Live Arts and Director of Operations of Ballroom Marfa. Additionally, she has worked with Fieldwork Marfa, Crowley Theater, Marfa Public Library, Marfa Contemporary, and The Contemporary (Austin). She currently serves on the board of Nameless Sound (Houston).

ANTHONY ELMS

Anthony Elms is the Daniel and Brett Sundheim Chief Curator of the Institute of Contemporary Art at the University of Pennsylvania. There he has organized the exhibitions *Cauleen Smith: Give It or Leave It* (2018), *Endless Shout* (2016–7), *Rodney McMillian: The Black Show* (2016), and *Christopher Knowles: In a Word* with writer Hilton Als (2015). Elms is also a writer and has coordinated several independent projects, including the *2014 Whitney Biennial* as one of the three curators. In all endeavors, his past as a musician continues to catch up with him, infiltrating his activities with broad, pooling arrhythmias.

JAMES FEI

James Fei moved from Taiwan to the US in 1992 to study electrical engineering. He has since been active as a composer and performer on saxophones and live electronics. Works by Fei have been performed by the Bang on a Can All-Stars, Orchestra of the S.E.M. Ensemble, MATA Micro Orchestra, and Noord-Hollands Philharmonisch Orkest. Recordings can be found on Leo Records, Improvised Music from Japan, CRI, Krabbesholm and Organized Sound. Compositions for Fei's own ensemble of four alto saxophones focus on physical processes of saliva, fatigue, reeds crippled by cuts, and the threshold of audible sound production, while his sound installations and performance on live electronics often focus on electronic and acoustic feedback. Fei has taught at Mills College in Oakland since 2006, where he is Professor of Electronic Arts.

PHILLIP GREENLIEF

Since his emergence on the west coast in the late 1970s, saxophonist/composer Phillip Greenlief has achieved international critical acclaim for his recordings and performances with musicians and composers in the post-jazz continuum, as well as new music innovators and virtuosic improvisers. He has performed with Wadada Leo Smith, Meredith Monk, Rashaun Mitchell, and They Might Be Giants. Albums include *Lantskap Logic* with Fred Frith and Evelyn Davis, *That Overt Desire of*

Object with Joelle Leandre, and *All at Once* with FPR (Frank Gratkowski, Jon Raskin, Greenlief). Recent residencies have included the Banff Center for Art and Creativity and Headlands Center for the Arts. His critical writing has been published in *Artforum*, *Open Space* (SFMOMA), and *Signal to Noise*.

ANNA HALPRIN

Since the late 1930s, Anna Halprin has been creating revolutionary directions for dance, inspiring artists in all fields. Through her students Trisha Brown, Yvonne Rainer, and Simone Forti, Anna strongly influenced New York's Judson Dance Theater, one of the seedbeds of postmodern dance. She also collaborated with such innovative musicians as Terry Riley, LaMonte Young, Morton Subotnik, and Luciano Berio, as well as poets Richard Brautigan, James Broughton, and Michael McClure. Defying traditional notions of dance, Anna has extended its boundaries to address social issues, build community, foster both physical and emotional healing, and connect people to nature. In response to the racial unrest of the 1960s, she formed the first multiracial dance company and increasingly focused on social justice themes. When she was diagnosed with cancer in the early 1970s, she used dance as part of her healing process and subsequently created innovative dance programs for cancer and AIDS patients. An early pioneer in the use of expressive arts for healing, she co-founded the Tamalpa Institute with her daughter Daria in 1978. Today, the Tamalpa ArtCorps program continues a vision close to Anna's heart: using dance as a healing and peace-making force for people all over the world.

CLAUDIA LA ROCCO

Claudia La Rocco's work explores hybridity and improvisation, moving between poetry, prose, and performance. Her books include the selected writings *The Best Most Useless Dress* (Badlands Unlimited) and the novel *petit cadeau* (published in print, digital, and live editions by The Chocolate Factory theater). With musician/composer Phillip Greenlief, she is animals & giraffes, an experiment in multidisciplinary improvisation that has released the albums *July* (Edgetone Records) and *Landlocked Beach* (with Wobbly; Creative Sources). She edited *I Don't Poem: An Anthology of Painters* (Off the Park Press) and *Dancers, Buildings and People in the Streets*, the catalogue for Danspace Project's PLATFORM 2015, for which she was guest artist curator. From 2005 to 2015, she was a critic and reporter for *The New York Times*, and she is Editorial Director of Open Space, the San Francisco Museum of Modern Art's live and online commissioning platform.

IAN LEWIS

Ian Lewis is a radio producer and filmmaker living in Marfa. His recent radio work includes the documentary *Dark Skies, Dark Energies*, which relates the West Texas fracking industry to the nearby Dark Energy astronomy experiment it threatens, and *Dial 3 to Admit Your Personal Failure*, a fictional governmental unemployment helpline for The Dig, a podcast from Jacobin magazine. In 2015, he created the late-night radio series *The Far West Texas Surf Report* for Marfa Public Radio. His short films have been screened by Ballroom Marfa, Houston Cinema Arts Society, London Surf / Film Festival, and Paris Surf & Skateboard Film Festival, among others.

ROBERT AIKI AUBREY LOWE

Robert Aiki Aubrey Lowe is an artist, curator, and composer who works primarily with, but not limited to, voice and modular synthesizer for sound in the realm of spontaneous music. Along with analog video synthesis works, he has brought forth an A/V proposal that has been a focus of live performance and installation/exhibition. The marriage of synthesis and the voice has allowed for a heightened physicality in the way of ecstatic music, both in a live setting and recorded. The sensitivity of analogue modular synthesis echoes the organic nature of vocal expression, which in this case is meant to put forth a trancelike state. Lowe's works on paper tend towards human relations to the natural/magical world and the repetition of motifs. As of late, Robert has also put more focus on composition for film, both in solo scoring and collaboration. Through collaboration, Robert has worked with Ben Russell, Ben Rivers, Sabrina Ratté, Rose Lazar, Nicolas Becker, Jóhann Jóhannsson, Tarek Atoui, Philippe Parreno, Evan Calder Williams, Ariel Kalma, Susie Ibarra, YoshimiO, Alexandra Wolkowicz, Biba Bell, ADULT., Hildur Guðnadóttir, and Rose Kallal, as well as many others.

ALVIN LUCIER

Born in 1931 in Nashua, New Hampshire, Alvin Lucier was educated in public and parochial schools in his hometown, the Portsmouth Abbey School, Yale and Brandeis, and spent two years in Rome on a Fulbright Scholarship. From 1962 to 1970, he taught at Brandeis, where he conducted the Brandeis University Chamber Chorus, which specialized in new music. In 1966, along with Robert Ashley, David Behrman, and Gordon Mumma, he co-founded the Sonic Arts Union. From 1968 to 2011, he taught at Wesleyan University where he was John Spencer Camp Professor of Music. Alvin Lucier lectures and performs extensively in Asia, Europe, and the United States. He has collaborated with John Ashbury (*Theme*) and Robert Wilson (*Skin, Meat, Bone*). His sound installation *6 Resonant Points Along a Curved Wall* accompanied Sol DeWitt's enormous sculpture *Curved Wall* in Graz and in the Zilkha Gallery, Wesleyan University, in January 2005. His *Canon* was commissioned by the Bang on a Can All-Stars, while *Music with Missing Parts*, a re-orchestration of Mozart's *Requiem*, premiered at the Mozarteum, Salzburg, in December 2007. In October 2012, *Two Circles*, a chamber work commissioned by the Venice Biennale, was premiered there by the Alter Ego Ensemble. In December 2013, *December 12th* was performed by the Ensemble Pamplemousse at the Issue Project Room, Brooklyn, while *Firewood* was performed in March 2014 by the Bang on a Can All Stars at Merkin Hall, New York. Alvin Lucier was awarded the Lifetime Achievement Award by the Society for Electro-Acoustic Music in the United States and received an honorary Doctorate of Arts from the University of Plymouth. In November 2011, Wesleyan University celebrated Alvin Lucier's retirement with a three-day festival of his works.

NINA MARTIN

Nina Martin, MFA, PhD, is a choreographer, pedagogue, dance theorist, and performer. Centered in the phenomena of perception, composition, and spontaneous movement states, her research springs from 40 years of embodied research and applied dance. Practiced internationally, Martin's dance systems *Ensemble Thinking* and *ReWire Movement Method* are examined in ongoing studies of populations living with cerebral palsy. Martin's creative and scholarly research has received funding in the US from the National Endowment for the Arts through six choreography fellowships, New York State Council on the Arts, New York Foundation for the Arts, Joyce-Mertz Gilmore Foundation, Meet the Composer/Choreographer Grant, Irvine Foundation (CA), Texas Commission on the Arts, and Texas Christian University where she is professor in the School for Classical & Contemporary Dance. Martin is an artist member of the Lower Left Performance Collective where cooperative inquiry is valued, and is Board President of Marfa Live Arts.

RASHAUN MITCHELL AND
SILAS RIENER

Since 2010, Rashaun Mitchell + Silas
Riener have created dance in response to
complex and active spatial environments:
often merging elements of fantasy,
absurdity, and quiet contemplation into
challenging multifaceted performances.
After working together in the Merce
Cunningham Dance Company, Mitchell
and Riener developed a keen interest
in the ways abstraction and representation
coincide in the body. Their collaborative
work takes many forms: from site-specific
installations, improvisational dances,
and traditional proscenium pieces to
highly crafted and intimate, immersive
experiences. Historical influences and
aesthetic forms collapse into a visually-
charged hybrid physical language.
Together, they have been part of the
Lower Manhattan Cultural Council's
Extended Life Dance Development
program, the New York City Center's
Choreographic Fellowship, and have been
Artists in Residence at the Maggie
Allesee National Center for Choreography,
EMPAC @ RPI, Mount Tremper Arts,
Wellesley College, Jacob's Pillow, and
Pieter Performance Space. Their work has
been presented at MoMA PS1 as part of
Greater New York in 2015; The Chocolate
Factory; New York Live Arts; Danspace
Project; REDCAT; Summer Stages Dance
at the Institute of Contemporary Art/
Boston; Walker Art Center; Museum of
Contemporary Art Chicago; On the
Boards; Brooklyn Academy of Music;
The Joyce Theater; and at SF MoMA.

CAITLIN MURRAY

Caitlin Murray is the Director of Archives
and Programs for Judd Foundation. In
this capacity, she has been responsible for
co-editing *Donald Judd Writings* (2016)
and *Donald Judd Interviews* (2019).
Murray is also a co-owner of the Marfa
Book Company, a bookstore, publishing
house, as well as a film, gallery and
performance space, and a Founder of 300

S Kelly St, an artist-run gallery space in
Marfa, Texas.

STEPHEN PETRONIO

Stephen Petronio is a choreographer,
dancer, and Artistic Director of the
Stephen Petronio Company. Petronio was
born in Newark, New Jersey, and received
a BA from Hampshire College in Amherst,
Massachusetts, where he began his
early training in improvisation and dance
technique. He was greatly influenced
by working with Steve Paxton and was the
first male dancer of the Trisha Brown
Dance Company (1979 to 1986). He has
gone on to build a unique career,
receiving numerous accolades, including
a John Simon Guggenheim Fellowship,
awards from the Foundation for
Contemporary Performance Arts, New
York Foundation for the Arts, an
American Choreographer Award, a New
York Dance and Performance ("Bessie")
Award, and a 2015 Doris Duke
Performing Artist Award.

ÉLIANE RADIGUE

Born in Paris, Éliane Radigue lived in
Nice in the South of France with her
husband, the artist Arman, before settling
in Paris after their marriage ended.
In the late 1950s, she started to archive
sounds: found materials taken from
her immediate environment. At that time,
twelve-tone and serial music inherited
from Schoenberg was widely influential,
but was, to her, "not satisfying in terms
of sound." Seeking an alternative, she
discovered the work of Pierre Schaeffer
through the radio, and soon after
began working at the Studio d'essai at
RTF (French Radio and Television
Broadcasting), which from 1957 to 1958
was directed by Pierre Schaeffer and
presided over by Pierre Henry. As
an intern she was "splicing, cutting, and
editing tapes." After stopping her
compositional work for a decade, a period
during which she raised her three
children, she returned to Paris in 1967–68

as Pierre Henry's assistant at the studio Apsome, working fourteen to sixteen-hour days on his major work *Apocalypse de J ean* (1968). In Paris she felt isolated: both Henry and Schaeffer were unsympathetic to her propositions. She finally found her "very tiny space" in the vibrant community of New York, following two visits. The first trip was in 1964–65 with Arman, during which she met James Tenney, a composer, music theorist, and pioneer of computer music who mentored her and introduced her to musicians such as Philip Corner, Philip Glass, and Steve Reich as well as the FLUXUS scene. Returning to New York in 1970–71, on Steve Reich's recommendation, she started a residency at New York University School of the Arts, where she began working with the Buchla Modular Synthesizer. At NYU, Radigue shared her studio with two American composers, Laurie Spiegel and Rhys Chatham, who introduced her to artists like La Monte Young, among others.

JANICE ROSS

Janice Ross, Professor in the Theatre and Performance Studies Department at Stanford University, is the author of four books including *Like A Bomb Going Off: Leonid Yakobson*; *Ballet as Resistance in Soviet Russia* (Yale Univ. Press, 2015); and *Anna Halprin: Experience as Dance* (UC Press 2007). She is the winner of the 2015 CORD Award for Outstanding Scholarly Research in Dance, a Guggenheim Fellowship, a Fulbright Scholar Fellowship, two Stanford Humanities Center Fellowships, a Memorial Foundation for Jewish Culture Fellowship, and a 2015 Israel Institute grant to Jerusalem. She is past president of the international Society of Dance History Scholars.

CATE COLE SCHRIM

Cate Cole Schrim is a therapist based in Tacoma, Washington. She currently provides intensive services to children and families, often utilizing creative modalities in clinical treatment. Prior to her clinical career, Cate worked for the nonprofit Marfa Live Arts, producing performing arts events and arts education programs (2014 – 2017). She has worked as an educator in Marfa and San Antonio, Texas. Cate studied Studio & Performing Arts at Bard College, received her Bachelor's in Linguistics from the University of Texas at Austin, and her Master's in Counseling from Sul Ross State University in West Texas. Cate is interested in the connection between creative expression and wellness.

IDA SOULARD

Ida Soulard is a writer, independent curator, and doctoral researcher in art history at ENS / PSL University and artistic director of Fieldwork Marfa, an international research-in-residence program in Marfa, Texas. With Fieldwork Marfa, she is leading an ambitious new program at the intersection of critical theory, spatial practices, and contemporary art. In 2011, she co-founded a series of seminars and workshops titled *The Matter of Contradiction* (2011–2013) and in 2012 co-initiated *Glass Bead*, an online journal and research platform. She currently teaches at Beaux-Arts Nantes Saint-Nazaire and is affiliated to HEAD-Genève.

SABRINA TARASOFF

Sabrina Tarasoff is an independent writer and critic based in Paris. During the mid-2010s Tarasoff earned a BFA at Parsons Paris while also acting as codirector of the independent exhibition space Shanaynay in Paris. She is a contributing editor at *Mousse Magazine* and writes regularly for *Artforum*, *Flash Art*, and *X-TRA Contemporary Art Quarterly*. Her writing dwells on the movement between popular culture, poetry, and art, with a particularly keen eye on the nebulous "poet gang" that formed around the Wednesday Night Poetry series at Beyond Baroque Literary

Art Center in Venice, California during the early 1980s. She also runs the Summer Room, an annual residency at Treignac Projet in Treignac, France.

WENDY VOGEL

Wendy Vogel is a writer, critic, and independent curator based in New York. Her work focuses on the legacies of feminism and how sexual politics interface with questions of class, race, and ability. A former editor at *Flash Art International*, *Modern Painters* and *Art in America*, her writing has appeared in a variety of publications, including *Artforum, art-agenda, The Art Newspaper, ArtReview, frieze*, and *Mousse Magazine*. She is a 2018 recipient of The Creative Capital | Andy Warhol Foundation Arts Writers Grant in Short-Form Writing. She received an MA from the Center for Curatorial Studies at Bard College and was a Critical Fellow in the Core Residency Program at the Museum of Fine Arts Houston.

INSTITUTIONS & PROGRAMS

Marfa Live Arts engages a diverse community through the performing arts, arts education, film, music, and other cultural arts programs. Marfa Live Arts celebrates and strengthens the cultural richness of the people of Big Bend, and enhances the area's tourist appeal through sophisticated programming featuring the talents of the region's own professional performers, dedicated amateurs, and international artists.

Fieldwork Marfa is the joint project of two major European art schools, Beaux-Arts Nantes Saint-Nazaire and HEAD-Genève, with a twofold mission of research and pedagogy. Based on the idea of a research-in-practice, Fieldwork Marfa is an international researcher-in-residence program dedicated to the practice of art in public space, critical approaches to landscape, and artistic projects based on field investigation methods. Residents are selected on the basis of the singularity of specific projects they present. This research-based program is bound to pedagogical projects and off-site workshops driven by the two art schools and various partners, including the partnership between Beaux-Arts Nantes Saint-Nazaire and The School of Art at The University of Houston.

DUST (Desert Unit for Speculative Territories) is an experimental research studio working at the intersections of spatial practice, critical theory, and contemporary art. DUST initiated in 2016 a three-year series of transdisciplinary seminars, lectures, events, and workshops. A project conceived and organized by Abinadi Meza (University of Houston) and Ida Soulard (Beaux-Arts Nantes Saint-Nazaire) and funded for three years by the Partner University Fund-FACE Foundation.

Unless otherwise noted, all images are documentation of *Marfa Sounding* (2016–2018) and are courtesy of the artists and *Marfa Sounding*. Image descriptions refer to place, date, and program specifics.

Cover
Audience arriving at Mimms Ranch for performance of Alvin Lucier's *I Remember Morty* (2016) and *Vespers* (1969), May 29, 2016. Photo by Sarah Vasquez.

pp. 17–24
Charles Curtis performing *I Remember Morty* (2016) at Mimms Ranch, May 29, 2016. Photo by Sarah Vasquez.

Rehearsal for *Vespers* (1969) at Mimms Ranch with Erik DeLuca, May 28, 2016. Photo by Jennifer Burris.

Rehearsal for *Vespers* (1969) at Mimms Ranch with Inès Elichondoborde, May 28, 2016. Photo by Jennifer Burris.

Inès Elichondoborde and Christine Olejniczak performing *Vespers* (1969) at Mimms Ranch, May 29, 2016. Photo by Sarah Vasquez.

Moon as seen from Fieldwork Marfa land in Antelope Hills, May 26, 2016. Photo by Francisco Staton.

Detail of *Sferics* (1981) installation at daybreak at Fieldwork Marfa land in Antelope Hills, May 27, 2016. Photo by Francisco Staton.

Early morning observers at *Sferics* (1981) at Fieldwork Marfa land in Antelope Hills, May 27, 2016. Photo by Francisco Staton.

Charles Curtis performing *Charles Curtis* (2007) and *Slices* (2002) at Crowley Theater, May 28, 2016. Photo by Sarah Vasquez.

p. 28
James Fei and Alvin Lucier listening to *Sferics* (1981) on Fieldwork Marfa land at Antelope Hills, May 27, 2016. Photo by Jennifer Burris.

pp. 50, 53, 58
Erik DeLuca, *The Poet Singers* (video stills), 2018. Courtesy of the artist.

p. 53
Left to right and top to bottom: radio on the island Viðey; two shacks in Snæfellsnes; transmitter at the Iceland University of the Arts; geodesic dome satellite in Reykjanesbær; detail of drawing by Ingólfur Arnarson; four images with details of *Imagine Peace Tower* (2007), a memorial by Yoko Ono; detail of *Tvísöngur* (2012) by Lukas Kühne.

p. 55
Left to right and top to bottom: detail of *Tvísöngur* (2012) by Lukas Kühne; Hotel Holt exterior; Hotel Holt interior; people on frozen Tjörnin; detail of construction site on Nauthólsvegur; three images with details of small church at Árbær Museum; detail of Richard Serra's *Áfangar* (1990); detail of Macy's Eiðar (2004) by Paul McCarthy and Jason Rhoades.

p. 58
Left to right and top to bottom: two images with details of Macy's Eiðar (2004) by Paul McCarthy and Jason Rhoades; Yule Goat outside Ikea in Garðabær; detail of Erik's home; three images with details of Roni Horn's *Vatnasafn/Library of Water* (2007); snow in countryside; radio tower in Snæfellsnes; old Naval Air Station in Keflavík.

p. 72
Alvin Lucier performing *I Am Sitting in a Room* (1969) at Crowley Theater, May 28, 2016. Photo by Sarah Vasquez.

pp. 83–90
Nina Martin leading a community dance

workshop at Crowley Theater, May 27, 2017. Photo by Jessica Lutz.

Stephen Petronio performing Anna Halprin's *The Courtesan and the Crone* (1999) at Crowley Theater, May 27, 2017. Photo by Jessica Lutz.

Stephen Petronio performing Anna Halprin's *The Courtesan and the Crone* (1999) at Crowley Theater, May 27, 2017. Photo by Jessica Lutz.

Detail of disco ball from untitled performance ("New Work") by Rashaun Mitchell and Silas Riener with Phillip Greenlief at Fieldwork Marfa land in Antelope Hills, May 28, 2018. Photo by Amitava Sarkar.

Silas Riener performing at Fieldwork Marfa land in Antelope Hills, May 28, 2018. Photo by Amitava Sarkar.

Rashaun Mitchell in foreground and Silas Riener in background performing at Fieldwork Marfa land in Antelope Hills, May 28, 2018. Photo by Jessica Lutz.

Rashaun Mitchell performing at Fieldwork Marfa land in Antelope Hills, May 28, 2018. Photo by Jessica Lutz.

Seated audience at untitled performance ("New Work") by Rashaun Mitchell and Silas Riener with Phillip Greenlief at Fieldwork Marfa land in Antelope Hills, May 28, 2018. Photo by Jessica Lutz.

p. 95
Audience led by saxophonist Phillip Greenlief to outdoor site for untitled performance ("New Work") by Rashaun Mitchell and Silas Riener at Fieldwork Marfa land in Antelope Hills, May 28, 2018. Photo by Jessica Lutz.

pp. 100, 105
Andrew Abrahams, *Returning Home* (video stills), 2003. Courtesy of the artist.

pp. 119-126
Jad Atoui with Fieldwork Marfa student at an open rehearsal held at Vizcaino Park, May 22, 2018. Photo by Jessica Lutz.

Ian Lewis activating Tarek Atoui's *0.9* (2016–) at Vizcaino Park public performance, May 27, 2018. Photo by Jessica Lutz.

Jad Atoui in foreground and *0.9* (2016–) performer Christine Olejniczak in background at Vizcaino Park, May 27, 2018. Photo by Jessica Lutz.

Amma Ateria performing at Vizcaino Park, May 27, 2018. Photo by Jessica Lutz.

Audience under moonlight at Vizcaino Park, May 27, 2018. Photo by Jessica Lutz.

Tarek Atoui activating the Athens *Sound Box* (2015) at Crowley Theater, May 25, 2018. Photo by Jessica Lutz.

Robert Aiki Aubrey Lowe performing at Crowley Theater, May 25, 2018. Photo by Jessica Lutz.

Audience in foreground with Tarek Atoui and passing cargo train in background at Saint George Hall public performance, May 26, 2018. Photo by Jessica Lutz.

p. 130
Audience in front of aluminum-roofed outdoor bandshell at Vizcaino Park public performance, May 27, 2018. Photo by Jessica Lutz.

p. 136
Amma Ateria performing at Saint George Hall, May 26, 2018. Photo by Jessica Lutz.

p. 157
Robert Aiki Aubrey Lowe performing at Crowley Theater, May 25, 2018. Photo by Jessica Lutz.

MARFA SOUNDING
2016–2018

Jennifer Burris, Co-Founder and Curator
Rob Crowley, Technical
JD DiFabbio, Co-Founder and Producer
Emma Rogers, Production Assistant
Ryan Rooney, Technical
Gory Smelley, Technical
Ida Soulard, Curator
Cate Cole Schrim, Production Assistant

Major support for *Marfa Sounding* was provided by Beaux-Arts Nantes Saint-Nazaire, City of Marfa, Étant donnés Contemporary Art – FACE Foundation, Kathrine G. McGovern College of the Arts at the University of Houston's Interdisciplinary Initiatives, Marfa Live Arts, MeyerSound, National Endowment for the Arts, Partner University Fund – FACE Foundation, Texas Commission on the Arts, and Texas Women for the Arts.

Additional and in-kind support was provided by The Big Bend Sentinel, Carl B. & Florence E. King Foundation, CineMarfa, The Chinati Foundation/ La Fundación Chinati, Crowley Theater, Dixon Water Foundation, DUST (Desert Unit for Speculative Territories), Fieldwork Marfa (and students), Marfa Book Company, Marfa Public Radio, Marfa Independent School District, Marfa Recording Co., Marfa Table, International Women's Foundation, Saint George Hall, and Vizcaino Park.

We would like to thank the following individuals for their generous advice, collaboration, and help: Rima Abdul-Malak, Oscar Aguero, Jessica Allen, Karen Ames, Claire Amiot, Laurent Auffret, Cody Barber, Yoseff Ben-Yehuda, Sam Cabos, Amandine Castillo, Lissa Castro, Crystal Catano, Sylvie Christophe, Tim Crowley, Erik DeLuca, Alan Dickson, Anne-Claire Duprat, Inès Elichondoborde, Charlotte Esnou, James Fei, Pierre-Jean Galdin, Mona Garcia, Fabien Giraud, Jean-Pierre Greff, Rob Gungor, Rae Anna Hample, Angel Hernandez, Paul Hunt, Marie Lozon de Cantelmi, Jennie Lyn Hamilton, Darby Hillman, Tim Johnson, Patrick Keesey, Ian Lewis, Minerva Lopez, Jeffrey Lubow, Philippe Manzone, Nina Martin, Lorne Matalon, Asa Merritt, Perrin Meyers, Abinadi Meza, Mary Mois, Ann Marie Nafzinger, Diana Nguyen, Christine Olejniczak, Elise Pepple, Simone Rubi, Linda and Don Schafer, Dan Shiman, Francisco Staton, Mai Tran, Cory Van Dyke, Emily Williams, and Leïla Zerrouki.

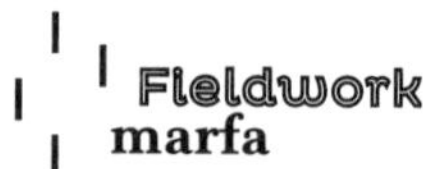

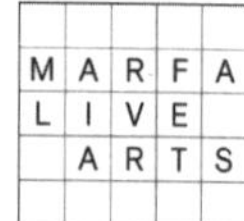

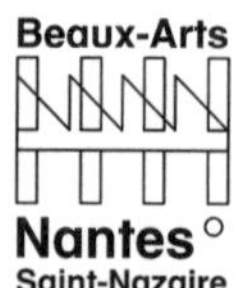

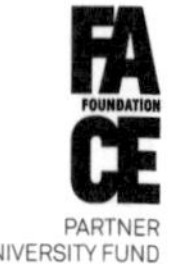

his book was published with support
om Athénée Press, Beaux-Arts Nantes
aint-Nazaire, and New Music USA.

dditional support from the School
 Art, Design, and Media at Nanyang
echnological University, Singapore,
ded the publication's development.

he following essays were reprinted with
ermission: "Tracks and Traces" by
brina Tarasoff, originally published in
ieze on June 30, 2016; "The Body Wants"
 Wendy Vogel, originally published under
e title "*Marfa Sounding*: Anna Halprin"
Performa Magazine on June 21, 2017;
d "The Poet Singers" by Erik DeLuca,
iginally published in *Public Art Dialogue*
2019, Vol. 9, No. 1, pp. 82–94. The
say "Compositions for Charles Curtis"
 Jennifer Burris was initially presented
 the National Gallery of Singapore
part of the public programming for the
hibition *Minimalism: Space. Light. Object*
ovember 16, 2018–April 14, 2019).
 other texts were commissioned for
s publication.

itors: Jennifer Burris and Ida Soulard
sign: Goda Budvytytė
py-editor: Maggie Jones
tography: Jessica Lutz, Amitava
kar, and Sarah Vasquez

images are documentation of
rfa Sounding (2016–2018) unless
ed otherwise.

lished and distributed by
usse Publishing
ntrappunto s.r.l.
rso di Porta Romana 63
22, Milan–Italy

ailable through:
usse Publishing, Milan
ussepublishing.com

P | Distributed Art Publishers, New York
ook.com